Fine...ly

My story of hope, love, and destiny

Randi G. Fine

"Fine...ly," by Randi G. Fine. ISBN 978-1-60264-649-0.

Published 2010 by Virtualbookworm.com Publishing Inc., P.O. Box 9949, College Station, TX 77842, US. ©2010, Randi G. Fine. All rights reserved. No part of this publication may be reproduced, stored in a retrieval system, or transmitted in any form or by any means, electronic, mechanical, recording or otherwise, without the prior written permission of Randi G. Fine.

Manufactured in the United States of America.

This book is dedicated with love:

To my devoted husband, Billy, who captured my heart forever, has stood faithfully by my side for twenty-two years, and has always believed in me.

To my precious daughter and son, Cammy and Kerry, who light up my life, fill my heart with joy, and overwhelm me with pride.

To my adored sisters, Marlene and Michele, who have loved, supported, and validated me throughout my life.

To my guardian angels, who with wisdom and dedication have allowed me to stumble, but have never let me fall.

To God, my infinite source of strength, guidance, and love.

Look to each day

With eyes of wonder

And let your ears

Bring to you its glory.

Look never to yesterdays

For you cannot change them,

Just let them guide you,

Remind you.

And let your dreams rise

To each new day's sun,

And be at one with yourself

~ Anonymous

Table of Contents

Acknowledgements

I'd like to dearly thank my gifted and talented editors, Joyce Sweeney and Cameryn Fine, for their invaluable expertise. Both of these outstanding women deserve credit for the honest and insightful guidance that they have provided me with during the writing process. Through Joyce's and Cammy's wisdom, I was able to shape my life story and transform it from a novice's first manuscript into a meaningful, impactful book.

I'd also like to thank and give credit to Helen Walker, a lovely and admirable friend, for wondrously conjuring up the perfect book title out of thin air.

Prologue

I believe that there are divine reasons for the pregnant pauses in our lives; the times when our life seems to come to a screeching halt and we are rendered powerless over it. Those are the times we should pay especially close attention, for those junctures may be the most profound times in our lives. Though painful, those intervals cause us to sit quietly and come face to face with our true selves. They provide tremendous opportunities for our spiritual growth.

Despair is a lonely, desolate place we've all visited at some point in our life. While in its depths it seems to take an immense amount of courage to reach for rose colored glasses and put them on.

I spent the first thirty years of my life as a pleaser, yielding to everybody else's expectations of me. Convinced that it was inconsiderate to ever put myself first, I continually dismissed my own needs. Having never developed a healthy self-esteem, I based my identity entirely on the ever-changing opinions of others and my interpretation of their reactions to me. My boundaries were undefined; I wavered between unfiltered vulnerability and impenetrable emotional walls. Those were very tumultuous and depressing years for me.

In my early twenties I met and fell in love with a recovering drug addict. I believed that if I loved him enough he would stay straight. But it wasn't long before that love turned into a painful, toxic obsession and I found myself trapped in the depths of despair.

Until I began to gain insight into where I had come from I couldn't capably decide where to go. I couldn't correct a problem that I had no understanding of in the first place. My awareness came by way of twelve-step group attendance, professional therapy, and a plethora of self-help books. The healing lavished upon me is a spiritual gift. Out of immense gratitude I want to pay it forward.

My aspiration through the sharing of my story is to offer hope, encouragement, and enlightenment to the millions of people who currently suffer alone in their darkness, lost in a maze of confusion and despair. My message is to hold on; that a brighter day is on the horizon.

For those who have already healed after living through experiences similar to mine, my hope is that they'll glean new insights from the benefit of a different perspective.

The stories that I reveal in this book are true and honest accounts. Most of my recollections are from memory or from letters, records and journals that I've kept over the years. Some names have been changed to preserve the person's anonymity. At the risk of being labeled "One Fruit Loop shy of a full bowl," I feel that I must also give due credit for the input that I received from "The Beyond." I believe without a doubt that much of the wisdom and some of the details from the past that had slipped my mind were imparted to me that way. Believe what you will.

I am thankful for everyone who has touched my life. I'm especially grateful to the people who have presented the most difficult challenges for me; I consider them to have been my most valuable teachers.

According to research conducted by professionals in the field of psychology, there are common threads that have been traced back to the childhoods of many adults who suffer from co-dependency. Many had been "pleaser" children who'd been conditioned from a young age to believe that they were only good or valuable when compliant with their parents' wishes. Often those wishes were illogical and confusing. As children they felt unduly responsible for their parents' needs and happiness. Healthy emotional boundaries between their parents and themselves were never properly established. They had often suffered from depression and/or anxiety in their adolescences, conditions that continued to trouble them well into adulthood.

The codependent syndrome develops over a long period of time. Those who suffer from codependency in their adulthoods have often had erroneously difficult adolescences. But they are largely unaware of their tendencies until their condition impedes their ability to form healthy, stable relationships.

I am grateful to say that although I suffered from that confusion for the first thirty years of my life, today, at fifty-two years of age, my life doesn't resemble that portrayal in any way. But remembering where I've come from keeps me humble.

It is my sincere hope that as you peruse the pages of my book you will find my story touching, inspirational, and most importantly an impetus for healing.

I wish you joy, serenity, and an abundance of love in your life.

One: Keith's Death

*For some moments in
life there are no words
~ David Selzer*

As we lay on our backs looking up at the sky, I glanced over at Cammy expecting to see a spark of childish wonderment in her eyes. She'd been a delight, as was typically her nature, but with the excitement of the evening I'd forgotten that it really was way past her bedtime. I could see that she was fighting the urge to sleep; her tiny eyelids looked heavy and kept drifting closed.

Almost an hour had passed since the first launching of the fireworks display. With a sense that the grand finale might begin at any moment, we made a split-second decision to pack up our camp and leave a few minutes early. With any luck we'd avoid the torrent of people all trying to exit the park at the same time, hopefully circumventing the impending traffic jam on the only road out of there.

We quickly grabbed our things and then proceeded to forge a pathway through the vast sea of spectators, trying to be as considerate as possible under the circumstances and not to trample on anyone's blanket. Feeling secure in the safety of her Daddy's arms, Cammy laid her sleepy head on his shoulder as we headed for our car.

As we drove home, I turned my head around and peered into the back seat of the Maxima. Not surpri-

1

singly Cammy was sound asleep, her head gently resting on the adult-sized seatbelt strap that miniaturized her petite stature by contrast. A perfectly spiraled golden curl lay softly over one eye. I found myself gazing at her for a moment, marveling at her untainted beauty. Though I dreaded the thought of ever having to disturb her, I knew that we'd be home in less than fifteen minutes. Surely she'd wake up as we transferred her from the car into the house.

"Daddy will carry you upstairs," I said as he lifted her languid, dazed, and glassy-eyed, out of the car. He carried her up the front walkway and into the house. "Brush your teeth and get ready for bed, then I'll come up to tuck you in and kiss you goodnight."

I stood in the foyer watching as they ascended the staircase. Then as I turned and faced the unlit kitchen straight ahead, the blinking red light on the answering machine that was sitting near the edge of the kitchen counter caught my eye. I felt it beckoning me with rapidly pulsating, imposing urgency. Curious, but with a sense of inexplicable foreboding, I approached the machine and played the message.

"Keith's dead. Call me as soon as you get home." Her tone of voice was stunningly matter-of-fact; she hadn't identified herself but she didn't need to. There was no mistaking the distinct, raspy sound of my ex-mother-in-law's voice…I knew it well.

Though predictable and imminent, the startling news railroaded me. Keith, my thirty-four year old ex-husband was dead.

The jolting impact of that day, Wednesday, July 4, 1990, would be indelibly pressed on my memory forever.

Two: Reminiscing

Experiences are indelibly written on the mind of a child...the parents are the master calligraphers.
~ *The Author*

I took my first breath of life on September 4, 1958. Two sisters, Marlene age seven and Michele age five preceded me in my family. My parents, already married eleven years, couldn't believe their good fortune. As far as they were concerned girls were the most precious gifts on earth. They were elated at the thought of adding a third daughter to their young family. I was well received; when Mom and Dad brought me home from the hospital my sisters were overjoyed. They'd been asking my parents for a baby sister.

Our Jewish middle class family of five lived comfortably, though not lavishly, in a suburb of Baltimore County called Pikesville. In the year of my birth my parents had purchased a modern, three-bedroom, split-level home in a development still under construction. The county, still mostly farmland, seemed like a million miles away from Baltimore City where they had lived out the first thirty years of their lives with everyone they'd ever known. It was quite a bold move for them at the time.

My father's well-reputed, second generation, family-owned dry cleaning business was among the finest in that area. My grandfather had unwittingly pulled my father, along with two of his brothers, into his tailor-

3

ing/dry cleaning business as a young man just out of the army. There were many other trades my father would have preferred but he hadn't been offered a choice or given a chance to pursue those interests. A conscientious provider for our family, he put in long hours and worked hard at a job that he found aggravating, stressful, and unrewarding.

Like the majority of married women of that era, my mother stayed at home taking great pride in her role of full-time housewife and mother. She was what Jewish people refer to as a *balabusta* (the yiddush word for "Susie Homemaker"). Mom was a fantastic cook and baker; she made a three–course, home-cooked dinner every night and baked all of her own cakes. She always looked well put-together with her crisply-pressed apron, her just-so hairdo, and her manicured, long nails. Our home was always clean and tidy.

By all appearances we were the model family. My sisters and I were immaculately dressed and perfectly posed from tallest to shortest with our feet pointing in the same direction in most every picture my father took of us. Mom always made sure our shoes were clean and polished. Because my father strived for nothing less than perfection each time he took our picture, my sisters and I associated tension with the photo sessions and dreaded them. I'm grateful to have the pictures to look back on, though candid shots would have given the same results with far less emotion attached to the experience.

My parents gave us every advantage that they could afford: music lessons, art lessons, dance lessons, etc. Dad planned fun or cultural family excursions almost every weekend and we took nice, week-long, family vacations together each summer.

They were an attractive couple who had a large social circle and were extremely well liked in the community.

My mother was a dedicated, dutiful daughter to her parents. She stayed very active in our synagogue's sisterhood, often serving on the board, and she generously volunteered her time whenever it was needed. She'd invite friends or family over for home-cooked dinners on the weekends, and almost all family holiday meals were hosted at our home.

Dad was a civic-minded man. He was energetic, organized, and helpful; always ready in his spare time to pitch in and lend a hand to those in need. He was passionate, outgoing, and outspoken when it came to most everything, mainly his political views. He'd often write letters to politicians or government officials to express his opinions, trying to improve society and change laws.

With my father at work and my sisters in school, my mother and I spent our weekday mornings and early afternoons together. Thinking back, I recall in vivid detail watching with renewed fascination each week as Mom's hairdresser teased and coifed her thick red tresses into a stiffly set "Beehive" hairdo. After her standing Friday morning Beauty Shop appointment we'd pick up a freshly baked, twisted poppy seed *challah* from Silber's kosher bakery for our traditional family Friday night *Shabbas* dinner. I'll never forget Silber's intoxicating bakery aroma and how much I looked forward to the chocolate filled, green or pink leaf-cookies nestled in waxed paper that the ladies would hand to me from behind the glass counter.

Another distinct memory I have from those years is of my mother and me at the neighborhood pharmacy one morning. We were standing just inside the doorway when a woman, someone my mother might have casually known, commented to her that I looked like a little *Shiksa* (the Yiddish name for a gentile girl). The woman's audacious *chutzpah* seems rude even now when I think about it, but having observed me at the time with my light blonde hair, green eyes, and turned up nose, her opinion was certainly understandable. I didn't possess *any* stereotypically Jewish features. When my mother retells the story now, she reminds me of how offended I was at that labeling. I'm not quite sure what I found insulting at the time. As a Jewish adult with the exact same features I proudly wear my *Shiksa* badge!

By nature I was a very shy and often moody child. From birth until age seven I was afflicted with an unexplained fear of men. My paternal grandfather rarely saw my face because it was often eclipsed by whatever arm I'd use to cover it. And if he spoke to me I'd dash behind the nearest chair or table leg and hide. With few exceptions the mere approach of a man would reduce me to tears. And I'd spontaneously recoil if one got close enough to touch me. I don't know why but I felt defiled by their attention. Certainly nothing inappropriate had ever happened to me at that early age. In hindsight, with no other reasonable explanation, I believe that my reaction was the result of a subconscious past life memory or future premonition...possibly both.

Though my sister Michele was a small child herself, she was unusually mature for her age. She enthusiastically took on the role of second mother to me. My mother fully trusted her to watch me, knowing that she'd keep me safe and entertained. When Michele was old enough, my mother would allow her to take me for walks around the block and even prepare simple meals for me. She burnt everything that she cooked for me, but I learned to love my food that way and still do to this day. I always looked up to her with adoration. She was my role model, advisor, teacher, and confidant.

My oldest sister Marlene, seven years my senior, wasn't nearly as involved in my life or as attentive during my childhood. I guess she couldn't relate to me because the gap between our ages was too wide. I had no doubt that she loved me; she was just busy with her own life and her own friends. And where Michele and I shared a bedroom, which probably contributed to our tight bond, Marlene always had her own room. Over the years, the age gap between us seemed to narrow and we became very close. As adults, my sisters and I are each others' best friends.

Three: The Contest

*Few of us write great no-
vels. All of us live them.
~ Mignon McLaughlin*

W hen I started first grade, both of my sisters were already attending Junior High
School. By the time my elementary
school years were winding down, Marlene had
started college and Michele was in her junior year of
High School. Having gone through their school
years basically back to back, they'd been taught by
some of the same teachers. I'd heard the names of
many of the teachers at Milford Mill High School
repeated, and through my sisters' after-school com-
mentaries I had a sense of their personalities.

When I answered the telephone in the kitchen
one afternoon and heard the voice of a friendly, nice
man claiming to be my sister's high school Biology
teacher, I didn't think twice about carrying on a
conversation with him. Since Marlene had already
graduated from high school, I just assumed he was
referring to Michele. I hadn't noticed at the time, but
he never actually said her name.

The man started the conversation by comment-
ing to me that my sister was one of his best students.
As far as I was concerned that statement validated
his authenticity; Michele was very smart and well
liked by all her teachers. Then he asked if I would
like to participate in a survey to help my sister win a

contest. Without pause I said yes, excited to hear all the details. So he continued, explaining that the survey would determine which of his students' younger siblings knew the most about the topic of sex. Understandably taken aback and extremely embarrassed by the subject matter, I hesitated.

The man immediately sensed my ambivalence and guilefully remarked that every other sibling he'd already spoken to had willingly participated. I believed that if I chose not to participate, my sister had no chance of winning; I didn't want her to be disappointed. So under the assumption that all the other kids had participated and handled the subject matter with maturity, I decided that I could too. I set my embarrassment aside and agreed to participate.

I stretched the coiled white telephone cord as far as it would go from the kitchen wall into the adjacent dining room so no one would overhear my conversation. Then I sat down on the carpeted floor, behind the dining room table, ready to begin.

Once the survey began, I felt terribly shameful as I quietly uttered my responses to his immodest questions. I certainly didn't want my mother to hear me saying those dirty words; she would not have understood. The man kindly encouraged me on, often complimenting my knowledge and reassuring me that I was doing well.

Before long the questions evolved into overtly personal inquiries; the man began asking for my responses to "tactile" directives. The things he was asking me to do were awful and I wanted to stop. But feeling bound by my commitment, I cooperated. Employing mind over matter, I remained focused on the ball. I'd come that far and I wanted to be sure that Michele would win the contest.

When it was finally over, the man told me that I had done an excellent job, he assured me of my sister's first place position, then he thanked me very much for participating and said goodbye.

I remained seated on the carpeted floor for a moment, the sound of the deep-pitched, droning dial tone resonating from my lap where the receiver lay. The embarrassing interrogation had left me feeling sullied, violated, and confused. I questioned my feelings, wondering if perhaps I just wasn't as mature as the other kids who took the survey had been. But after all things considered I still felt proud that I'd gotten through it and done well. I knew how grateful Michele would be when she found out that she'd won the contest.

I sat there sorting out the conundrum for a minute or so before I stood up, hung the receiver back on the kitchen wall, and went on with the rest of my day.

At six o'clock that evening my family of five sat down at the kitchen table for dinner. Just as we did every night we discussed the goings on of our days, each of us anxiously awaiting the chance to chime in with our comments. I finally got the floor, turned to Michele and excitedly said, "Your teacher called today. He said I did a really good job. He said that you definitely won!"

Michele looked at me inquisitively and asked, "What teacher?"

"You know," I answered in an upbeat but matter of fact tone. "He called about the contest."

"What contest?" she asked me curiously.

I pressed on, trying to be as discreet as possible. "*You* know…the *contest*…?"

"No I *don't* know! What are you *talking* about?" she asked, annoyed.

"You know…the *sex* contest!" I blurted out. I glanced over at my mother and saw the color rapidly draining from her face.

"We aren't *having* any contest" my sister replied, now noticeably concerned.

Everyone stopped eating, all eight eyes focused on me. My mind flashed back to the shameful proceedings of that day; my entire being felt filthy and contaminated.

My mother shouted "Oh my God! I'm calling the police!" *Oh, great!* The last thing I wanted to do was recap the details of that mortifying experience; I already felt exceedingly stupid and colossally embarrassed.

What would I say? How could I explain what happened? The topic of sex had never been discussed in our home; I dreaded the thought of having to be the first one in the family to talk about it. I wanted to cut and run. Or fold my arms, blink my eyes, and funnel my vapors into a nearby bottle like Barbara Eden did on *I Dream of Jeannie.*

Unfortunately I was still present and physically intact when an officer knocked at our front door. My mother invited him inside to take an incident report. As I'd dreadfully anticipated, lots of sensitive questions were asked that required responses only I could answer. I felt violated all over again.

The officer quipped as he was leaving, that finding the perpetrator of a crime like that was like looking for a needle in a haystack. Clearly the pervert that had so brazenly marred my innocence would never be caught or identified.

Although I was unnecessarily tainted, I quietly dealt with my feelings as best I could and moved on. My badly shaken mother never spoke of the incident again.

Four: The Golden Child

*To look backward for a while
is to refresh the eye, to restore it, and to render it the
more fit for its prime function of looking forward.*
~ *Margaret Fairless Barber*

My parents did many wonderful things for me and my sisters over the years. We'll never forget the gifts we've been given, the many opportunities we've been offered, our parents' personal sacrifices, and the kindness we've been shown. The three of us will always be immensely grateful for all those things. With that said, the truth is that no amount of kindness could *ever* counteract the devastating effects of *years* of their emotional abuse. To this day, the three of us are still untangling the mess they made.

When I was a child, my mother would often comment to me that she hoped I'd develop a "thicker skin" then she had. That always confused me. I wondered how she planned to give me the tools to develop strength and resiliency when she could never attain those skills herself.

From a very young age I had an innate curiosity about what life outside of my family was like and how other people experienced it. I knew that my mother was unable to broaden my perspective on life. She lived safely inside of her middle class

Jewish bubble and wanted her children to do the same. My father, who had served in World War II as a medic on the front lines and had seen the heinous atrocities that mankind was capable of, was fiercely protective of my mother. He intently kept her in that bubble and allowed her to rule the roost from that limited, maybe even skewed vantage point.

To be fair she wasn't unlike many other Jewish people who, feeling justified in their suspicion that every other human being on the planet was Anti-Semitic, had formed a cohesive inner circle. They had tragically lost six million of their people in the despicable, senseless holocaust.

My parents, both born in the 1920's, had grown up with a generation of parents that believed children should be seen and not heard. The parents of that era demanded respect, whether or not that respect was warranted or reciprocated. Children were dutiful and compliant or suffered the consequences. They did what was expected of them and never complained. The average person knew nothing about psychology or discussed their feelings; they just stockpiled their pain. Guilt was believed to be a great motivator.

My father had grown up without ever knowing his mother--she had died when he was five years old. In his eyes, a mother was a queen up on a pedestal. On more than one occasion over the years, Dad has wished me or one of my sisters a happy birthday and then urged, "Thank *Mother* for giving birth to you." The inflection in his voice always indicated that he thought it would be rude *not* to give her credit and *not* to focus on *her.* He completely disregarded the fact that our birthday was the only day of the year that belonged to *us* and made *us* special—not Mom! He never had the slightest awareness of the inappropriateness of his suggestion. Mom ate the royal treatment up with a spoon.

Mom and Dad always said that they loved me and my sisters and would do anything for us. We believed what our parents would tell us, but in our hearts we knew that we came second to their relationship. If all five of us were in a boat drowning, we knew that Dad would definitely save our mother first. She always came first. He couldn't live without her; in his eyes she was perfection personified.

Dad always referred to Mom as "Mother," or "Your Mother." I don't ever remember him referring to her casually as Mom or Mommy. Likewise, whenever Mom wanted attention or demanded respect she would refer to herself in the third person. She'd say something like, "Your Mother is not feeling well." I was always tempted to reply, "Oh, she isn't?" But she forbid us to ever refer to her as "She." She'd become furious and say, "I am not a *SHE,* I am your *MOTHER!*"

Mom and Dad often told me and my sisters that they'd always be there for us—they said that we could tell them anything. But deciding whether or not to confide in them was always a hard call. Mom would be gentle, sympathetic, and understanding at the time, but then she'd often stew and use our disclosure against us at a later time, or repeatedly throw it in our face for years to come. And talking to Dad was useless because he'd tell Mom everything we said. We had no one to advocate for us, no one we could trust.

My parents never acted as a parental unit. A visual representation of our family structure would consist of three concentric circles—Mom in the center (the queen of the castle), Dad in the middle ring encircling her (the protective moat), and the children in the ring around him (the commoners).

Mom tended to use guilt tactics to elicit the compliance of her three daughters. She took everything we did or said personally; like our misbehaviors or emotional growing pains were intended to deliberately hurt her. If we did something wrong, which all children do, both of our parents would be sure to let us know how badly we had hurt Mom. That's a cruel and heavy burden to place on any child.

My sisters and I were often told to "do the right thing." That never made sense to me. What was "the right thing?" I always wondered if a universal understanding even existed; if the rules to follow were actually written in a book somewhere and if everyone in the world knew them.

From my mother's viewpoint, our family image and how it directly reflected upon her were of primary importance. She always worried about what other people would think. Mom's public persona was entirely different than her private one--she was a chameleon. Unaware that it was a façade, mostly everyone that she met or socialized with adored her. She thrived on that adoration and knew exactly how to obtain it.

My mother frequently and shamelessly belittled my father in the presence of me and my sisters. She'd often condemn his effectiveness as a father, knowing that it would guilt him into blindly fighting her battles for her. He was her puppet and she pulled the strings. Witnessing the deprecation sickened us, and it was pathetic to watch Dad being emasculated and relenting to the humiliation. It was so hard to respect them; they acted like children.

My parents each claimed, and quite often I might add, that no one had a spouse as wonderful as they did. But witnessing the dynamics of their relationship within the confines of our home, one would have assumed that they despised each other. My parents, though very devoted and outwardly affectionate to one another, argued all the time. Behind closed doors our home was an angry battleground. Their arguments were thunderous and heavy-laden with painful, lingering emotion.

As a young child I found the frequent upheaval distressing and frightening; in fact it was unbearable. Time stood still as I'd watch in silence and cower with my insides trembling, or stop whatever I was doing and listen nervously from another room, praying for their fighting to end. It tore me up inside; I often worried that they would get a divorce. Incredibly, that never happened. My parents never seemed to think they were doing anything wrong. I don't think they *ever* realized the impact that their insane behavior was having on their three impressionable children. If they did, that realization never stopped their despicable behavior; they were much too caught up in each other.

Physical, mental, and emotional boundaries were ignored in our family. My sisters and I were never permitted to lock or even close our bedroom doors. My parents viewed that as an insult—they wanted full access all the time. We could never create a barrier to escape from the madness without the risk of angering our parents even more or having Dad impetuously remove the door knob. When I became a defiant teenager, if my father would remove the door knob to my room, I'd locate and reinstall it myself while he was at work.

Besides being riddled with guilt that we had or would hurt Mom, my sisters and I jumped through ever changing hoops to avoid upsetting her. My mother liked pleasers, compliant children. She wanted all three of her daughters to fit inside the molds she'd made for them. Anything outside of those confines was unacceptable. When my sisters and I in turn reached our adolescence years and began the natural process of developing as individuals, Mom's anger intensified.

Mom assigned lifetime roles to each of her three daughters and treated us each differently: Marlene was the incorrigible rebel, Michele was the overly-sensitive scapegoat, and I was the do-no-wrong golden-child. We always felt as if we had three entirely different mothers. Each of our roles came with a heavy price to pay.

Sometimes when my mother was angry or frustrated with my sisters she'd resort to hurtful name calling, using words like "dumb-ox" and "phony."

She didn't seem to have the slightest care or awareness of the resonating impact of her words or how
they'd be imprinted on her daughters' developing
psyches forever. Since I was the baby of the family
and clearly my mother's favorite, I was immune to
the name calling until I entered adolescence. But
the abuse might as well have been directed at me
the entire time; I adored my sisters and couldn't
bear to see them hurt.

Mom never admitted to doing anything wrong.
In fact, she'd often deny that anything she did ever
happened. Who was going to advocate for us or tell
her otherwise? It would certainly not be Dad; he
thought she walked on water. Along with all the
other emotional abuse, that discrediting, deceptive
tactic made me and my sisters feel crazy, confused,
and insecure. On the rare occasions when Mom did
apologize, she'd say something like, "I'm sorry if
you're upset." She never took personal responsibility for her actions.

No matter what my sisters and I did with our
lives outside the home, and whatever decisions we
made, we were never to forget that Mom was the
center of our world and pleasing her was of the
utmost importance. Mom expected that devotion,
though she'd never admit it, and since Dad wor-
shiped the ground she walked on, he saw things no
other way. We found it very difficult to separate
from Mom at the appropriate stages of our development without feeling terribly guilty about hurting her. It's no wonder that my sisters and I became
unruly, defiant teenagers in our parents' eyes.
There was no healthy way for us to disentangle

from the stifling enmeshment of our family and blossom into the individuals that we had every right to be.

Hysterical crying that lasted for hours upon hours and loud door-slamming were common occurrences in our household. The slightest issues were over-emotionalized; our home was a place of frequent outbursts and melodramatics. Every argument escalated to the nth degree. I found it impossible to ever relax because I never knew when the next volcano would erupt.

It was terribly confusing because what my sisters and I saw with our eyes and felt in our guts didn't correlate with what our parents constantly lead us to believe. Our home life was one of smoke and mirrors. The inconsistency, unreliability, and unpredictability of our childhoods made each of us feel like we were forever in a state of insanity.

As the golden-child I was always expected to look perfectly and act perfectly. My mother idolized me and would give me the world on a silver platter when I played that role; she'd trample *anyone* who got in her way--including my father. But God help me when I couldn't fill those shoes.

As the youngest child I had the benefit of observing my sisters' interactions with our mother and learning from their mistakes. I discovered early on that the best way to keep the peace and stay on Mom's good side was to avoid certain topics, to say what she wanted to hear, to do things the way she wanted them done, and never ever worry her. Mom's worry was a catalyst for her anger. Out of sheer necessity I learned how to lie.

Clearly I was a "pleaser child." Desperate for serenity and harmony I served as the family peacemaker. Even as a very young child I'd assume the role of the family mediator, try to apply logic to illogical situations, and calm everyone down. The raging storm would eventually blow over but I'd remain traumatized from all the turmoil. I kept it all inside; no one knew what I was going through. I always had stomach issues.

I watched my mother constantly beat herself up, worry, and obsess over unimportant things that she'd encounter outside of our family. Since she was my primary female role model and she had no coping skills, I learned to react to the challenges of ordinary life in the same unhealthy manner. With no other coping methods to call on, I began building emotional walls inside of me as a fortress to protect me from all the insanity that surrounded me.

Children learn what they live. As the years passed, I became very proficient at protecting everyone else's feelings at my own expense. Conflict of any nature terrified and sickened me. "Pleaser" became my new middle name--I lived it and breathed it for the first forty years of my life.

Five: The Dream

From the beginning of time, doors have symbolically or literally represented places of danger or safety. The door is also representative of finding ones way through life. Situations involving doors have been prevalent themes throughout my life story.

I never felt safe in the house I grew up in. For one thing there were too many windows. Floor to (almost) ceiling windows covered seventy-five percent of one wall on the main floor of our house. A door that led out to the patio divided that window wall into two sections. Though the window wall was often covered by drapes, I felt too visible, too accessible; like anybody could watch me at anytime.

I used to have recurring nightmares about a dark, shadowy figure chasing me around the backyard and right up to the patio door where those windows were. Many of my childhood dreams involved our home's doors or windows.

My father had meticulously secured all the doors in the house with deadbolts, chains and/or slide bars, but I never saw the fortification as much of deterrence. Anyone could have walked right up to one of our many windows, thwacked the glass with a hammer, and crawled right in. That always worried me. We never had an alarm system.

Our house had four entry ways. Our family most frequently used the door in the carport that entered into our den. The front door was used mainly for guests. We used the patio door when we wanted to sit outside or go into the back yard, and the laundry room door was mainly used just to take out the trash.

The longest running, recurring dream I ever had involved that house and those doors. The dreams began in my adolescence and continued into my early forties.

In the dream I'm always standing by one of the four doors. My father is leaving so I am saying goodbye to him. Since I'll be home alone, I ask him to please make sure the door is securely locked. He assures me that he is deadbolt locking the door and that I'll be very safe. He tells me that I have nothing to worry about. I trust him at his word, he leaves, and I walk away.

I start feeling scared later on so I come back to check the lock and to relieve my mind. But when I touch the door knob with no effort at all, the door swings wide open. I try to relock it from the inside, but no matter what I do I can't secure the door; it keeps swinging open. I am left feeling vulnerable and imperiled.

When my father returns home, he finds me waiting by the door. I've been sitting there policing the door ever since I discovered the broken lock. I tell him how afraid I've been, knowing that someone could have easily broken in and hurt me. He doesn't understand what I mean. He says there's nothing wrong with the lock and then demonstrates the mechanism to prove it. The door locks perfectly for him. Unable to convince him to repair the deadbolt, since he sees nothing wrong with it, I remain fearful.

I can't begin to estimate how many times I had that dream over the years. My subconscious was obviously trying to work something out. The more I began to untangle the confusion of my childhood, the clearer the meaning of the dream became.

The dream speaks volumes about the vulnerability and lack of emotional safety I felt as a child. I know that my father truly believed he'd done everything in his power to protect his family. Unfortunately, I never felt secure or emotionally protected by either one of my parents. If they had no mastery over their own emotions, how could they possibly safeguard or nurture mine?

After working with a therapist for well over a year to understand and heal my childhood pain and other issues that had taken hold of me, I learned how to establish healthy boundaries with my parents and in every aspect of my life. I let go of the guilt and my need to please; two things that had handicapped me throughout my life. The dreams stopped when the therapy was completed. I was forty-two.

To this day my parents refuse to admit to or take any responsibility for their actions, past or present. Now they use their old age and ailments to hide behind. But it really doesn't affect me one way or another whether or not *they* accept any responsibility. I assumed the responsibility and healed *myself!*

My relationship with my parents today is very different than it had been for most of my life. I've come to accept that they are who they are and I've accepted myself for who I am. I please when I choose to please, not out of guilt or expectation. As adults, acceptance is our own responsibility and what healing is all about.

Six: The Homework Assignment

*I have never let my schooling
interfere with my education.*
~ Mark Twain

I was eleven years old in 1969 when I began sixth grade at Sudbrook Middle School. My class made history by being the first sixth grade to ever attend that school. Prior to that year, Sudbrook had been classified as a junior high school. The middle school movement was a fairly new concept in education for the Baltimore County school system in the late sixties.

Though still sort of shy I was beginning to like boys. I don't know what I actually liked about them; most of the boys my age were rude, awkward, and oblivious to girls. And often when a boy did like a girl he would show it by making her life a living hell. I had more than my share of that kind of attention. Some boys were "mature" enough to have girlfriends at that age. I definitely wasn't ready to be one of them. But there were a few cute boys in the mix that I found "crush worthy."

Since I had excelled academically throughout Elementary School I had been placed in all accelerated level classes for sixth grade. I can't recall the names of any of my teachers that year, with the exception of one...my English teacher, Mr. Faulkner.

In appearance, speech, and demeanor Mr. Faulkner had the classic traits that one would associate with a literary professor. He challenged his students to stretch their minds and elicited great respect from them.

The reason that Mr. Faulkner stands out so clearly in my mind has nothing to do with his teaching style. I remember him because he inappropriately crossed the line with me.

One day, while all the students in my class were working independently, Mr. Faulkner called me over to his desk. As I approached, he motioned for me to stand next to him. Then in a very quiet voice he asked me, "Do you know how sultry you are?" I figured that he was just challenging my intellect in his usual way so I innocently told him that I had no idea what that word meant.

Still speaking softly he said, "When you get home from school today, look up the word sultry in your dictionary. Consider that an extra credit assignment for tonight and tell me what the definition is in class tomorrow." He wrote the word down on a piece of loose-leaf paper and handed it to me.

I thought it was so cool that he'd singled me out. I considered it an honor to have the attention of such a well-admired teacher focused entirely on me. After having had my curiosity sparked I couldn't wait to learn the meaning of the new vocabulary word. As soon as I got home from school that day I went directly to the dictionary to look up the definition.

The Miriam Webster dictionary defined the word sultry as "oppressively hot and moist." I don't remember noticing any other definitions for that word, though now as an adult I know differently. The dictionary explanation as I interpreted it that afternoon baffled me. *I was hot and moist? What did that mean?* I couldn't understand the meaning of the word in the context he had used it. I wrote down the definition on the piece of loose-leaf paper to hand in anyway, but knew I'd have to wait for clarification of the meaning the next day.

Just before English class the following day I approached Mr. Faulkner. While handing him back the sheet of paper with the odd definition written on it I said, "Mr. Faulkner, I looked up the word sultry in the dictionary last night but the definition didn't make any sense to me. The dictionary defined the word as, 'hot and moist.' "I'm hot and moist? Is that what you're saying?"

He looked up from his desk chair and smiled at me, probably thinking my comment was cute or maybe even funny. Then he answered me in a hushed voice, "Sexy. It means you are very sexy." My skin began to crawl.

Yeeuck! Did that old fart just make a pass at me? Not knowing how to react, my first instinct was to shout back at him "You're really gross!" But too intimidated by him to actually respond that way, I managed to force a smile of embarrassment, pivoted my sultry little eleven-year-old tush around, and strolled over to my desk.

I don't know what he could have possibly thought he'd get out of telling an eleven year old girl that she was sexy.

That turned out to be an isolated incident; he never crossed the line with me again. And after taking it upon myself to assess the damage he'd caused to me as minimal, I decided not to turn our private little matter into a major fiasco. I certainly did not want to upset Mom...and I never told another soul.

But that was the second time I'd been subjected to inappropriate sexual advances by a grown man. I began to wonder if the gut feeling I'd had since I was a little girl had been accurate; that all men really did view me in a lewd way. No wonder they all creeped me out!

I began examining myself trying to connect all the dots. I knew that people thought I was a pretty girl because I'd often been complimented on my appearance and my mother always told me I was. There was nothing wrong with getting *appropriate* attention for that. But at eleven years old, I didn't believe that I was oozing with sexuality; then again, maybe I was. I wondered if perhaps, though unaware, I inherently possessed some kind of irresistible animal magnetism.

At any rate, I was too immature to sort out those thoughts in a healthy way. Since I didn't understand why it kept happening, I turned it on myself. I began feeling acutely conspicuous and self-conscious. The analogy that immediately comes to mind relates to the character Truman from the movie *The Truman Show*; how hyper-aware he became after realizing that his every move was being watched. Yes, that's it. I felt just like that.

For the next ten years, I'd have more than a few opportunities to affirm my poor self-image.

Seven: Escape at Reisterstown Road Plaza

> *Cunning is the art of conceal-*
> *ing your own defects, and*
> *discovering the weakness of*
> *others.*
> *~ William Hazlitt*

My parents often went out socially on the weekends, so in the years before I was old enough to stay home alone, I often slept over my maternal grandparents' house. My *Bubbe* and *Zaide* lived in a brick row house in Baltimore City, just on the outskirts of the county line. Their neighborhood was quiet, safe, and predominantly Jewish. Neither of my grandparents had ever learned to drive. Because they were very religious, and just as importantly for convenience sake, they lived within walking distance of shopping centers, kosher markets, and their synagogue.

The biggest shopping center in that area, The Reisterstown Road Plaza, was located only three blocks from their house. "The Plaza" as it was commonly referred to, was an open-air complex anchored by two department stores, Stewart's and Hecht Co., and lined with a variety of other stores. One could consider The Plaza the daytime social hub of that area. Senior citizens that lived in nearby neighborhoods often met there in the afternoons and congregated at tables or benches in the center of the plaza. Teenagers often spent their Saturdays hanging out there and shopping with friends, just as they do at malls today.

After I turned eleven, my grandparents allowed me to take the short walk from their house to The Plaza alone. I felt very independent and mature with that freedom. I also felt safe; my parents had drilled the usual lectures about not talking to strangers into my head. Besides, there had recently been an abduction and murder of a girl my age not far from there. That really hit home, so I was tuned in, and wary.

By myself at the Plaza one Saturday afternoon, looking through stacks of blue jeans in a store, an unfamiliar man in his forties approached me. He was nicely groomed with a seemingly affable personality. Having gotten the vibe that he'd been watching me and had established that I was alone, I ignored his initial attempts to speak to me. Although I didn't acknowledge his presence I listened to every word he said.

The man introduced himself as a Baltimore City, undercover detective. He claimed that he and his partners were about to execute a drug bust right outside of the store we were in and kindly asked me not blow his cover. He emphasized the importance of their mission. He inched uncomfortably close to me, then with his face right beside my ear, he imparted in a hushed voice that he needed a civilian decoy in order to proceed with the arrest.

I wasn't buying his obviously fabricated story so I finally spoke up and asked him to leave me alone. My response had little effect; it didn't seem to dampen his determination to speak to me in the least.

The "detective" commented that he'd been observing me and was very impressed with my apparent maturity. He said that he'd selected me because he thought I'd be the perfect decoy: the drug dealer would never suspect that a child would have any involvement with the police. He emphasized that I'd be in no danger whatsoever; I'd only serve as a distraction while the sting operation went down.

I told him, much more forcefully this time, to leave me alone. Still he persisted. He said that he understood why I didn't believe him; that his story must have sounded far-fetched. But he promised that he could prove his claim. All I had to do was stand at the front door of the store with him so he could show me something.

Thinking back, I'm not sure why I didn't enlist someone's help. Surely there were sales people or other customers who I could have turned to. But he had specifically asked me not to reveal his identity. And though I was suspicious of the man and his questionable motives, something about his story intrigued me, though I didn't let on.

This just illustrates how influential manipulators can be over a child and how even cautious and wary children become coerced into abduction.

Anyway, hoping to get rid of him, I finally agreed to stand with him at the front door. But that was all; I made it clear that under no circumstance would I leave the store or the confines of The Plaza with him.

The "detective" stood just outside the doorway, discreetly pointing to two plain-clothed men standing directly across the plaza. He whispered to me that they were the partners he had mentioned earlier who were also involved in the drug dealer's apprehension. Then the strangest thing happened; the men actually acknowledged his subtle gesture by nodding back at him.

After the astonishment of seeing their interchange, I immediately began to doubt my instincts. I even felt slightly guilty for my distrust. On second glance, he certainly seemed to be a legitimate officer of the law. I was led to believe that I could always trust policemen.

Sensing that he might have finally weakened my resolve, he pressed harder with his attempts to persuade me. "Now do you believe that I'm telling you the truth? I promise that I wouldn't lie to you. Please, we really need your help."

Although he had succeeded in confusing me, my better judgment still ruled. I shook my head from side to side and replied, "No. I'm sorry but I really can't."

Still persisting he suggested, "Let's walk down the Plaza to Read's drugstore together. No need to worry, we'll stay inside the shopping area the entire time. I'll buy you a Coke and explain everything. Okay?"

I was so confused. I wondered if I had unfairly misjudged the nice man. I thought about the amount of visible time he'd already spent with me. *Surely enough people had already seen us together and we'd have a lot more exposure as we headed for the drugstore.* Logically, it seemed to me that a kidnapper would not want to gamble with such high risks of being later identified. Believing it was a reasonably safe decision I took a giant leap of faith and agreed to hear him out.

As a main destination in the plaza, Read's drugstore drew many people. I'd been to the store more times than I could count, so I knew that Read's had two entrances and exits, one from inside The Plaza and a backdoor that led out to the parking lot. As we walked there side by side, I reiterated my conviction that under no circumstance would I leave the shopping center with him. He swore that he had no reason to even ask me to.

When we safely arrived at Read's as he'd promised, we walked to the back, sat down on the black-padded, chrome stools at the lunch counter, and ordered two fountain sodas. He attempted to carry on a friendly conversation with me while we sipped our Cokes. Trying to listen for clues that might indicate his true intentions, I said very little back to him.

As he nonchalantly continued trying to find out more about me, he gradually segued into mentioning that he'd parked his police car in the parking lot right outside of the drugstore. He off-handedly offered to show it to me, "if I had any interest." My red flag shot up like an arrow. His comment didn't make any sense to me; he had just finished swearing to me that he'd have no reason to ask me to go outside.

Suddenly it became clear to me that he wasn't a police detective, he wasn't nice, and that my life was in danger. He'd intended all along to lure me outside. No longer second guessing my better judgment, I promptly reached into my purse and took out a dime. I told the man that I just realized I was supposed to have called my mother; that it was time for her to pick me up.

Finally accepting his defeat, he paid the check, thanked me for my time, then stood up and disappeared out the back door to the parking lot.

With the reality of what could have happened to me thrashing around in my head, I sat paralyzed on the bar stool. It terrified me to think that he might return. After I'd sat frozen there for a few minutes I began to worry that he might be waiting somewhere else in the Plaza for me; that he'd find and kidnap me.

Finally accepting that I couldn't sit on that stool forever, and aching to get back to the safety of my grandparents' house, I finally mustered up enough courage to stand up and dash from the back of Read's to the front door that led out into the shopping center. Cracking open the doorway just enough to crane my head out, I looked every which way twice. Feeling confident enough to make my daring move, I scurried out of the door and through the plaza, frequently looking back over my shoulder. Once I reached the parking lot I high-tailed it back to my grandparents' house. When I finally caught my breath, I casually walked back into their house as if nothing was wrong.

Since I ultimately had suffered no harm and didn't want to worry or upset anyone, especially my mother, I never mentioned the incident.

Eight: The Accident

If you look closely at a tree you'll notice its knots and dead branches, just like our bodies. What we learn is that beauty and imperfection go together wonderfully
~ *Matthew Fox*

W hen I think of my early childhood years, those three episodes, which all happened to involve older men, stand out the clearest in my mind. Even today a nauseating feeling overtakes me when I think about those events. Though I remained physically unscathed for the most part, my budding self-image did not. Experience continued to shape my belief that my most valuable assets were my ability to please and pacify, and my appearance.

By age eleven I'd begun to understand why my mother insulated herself from the real world and wanted her children to do the same; life was perilous and people were deviant. But I couldn't see living the rest of my life in a bubble like my mother did. I knew that if I wanted to experience life as I believed it was meant to be experienced, the sooner I hardened myself emotionally the better off I'd be in the long run. With that determination I began to seek out problematic people and often put myself in questionable situations to test my fortitude.

Believing that my mother couldn't effectively handle my problems, I came to the realization that I really didn't have anybody but myself to lean on.

Throughout my childhood and teenage years, whenever I expressed feelings of sadness (and I often did), my mother would attempt to console me by saying "Why are you depressed? You have nothing to be unhappy about. You're beautiful!"

All I can say is that she truly meant well. But those words just reaffirmed to me that my intelligence and talents didn't factor into the equation. Convinced that one of my strongest assets was a perfect appearance, I conditioned myself to never accept less. I believed that if I didn't look perfect and act perfect, no one would love me. And since perfection is virtually impossible to achieve, one can well imagine the pain I repeatedly inflicted upon myself. I'd turn on myself every time my appearance didn't get me what I wanted.

Without the foundation of a healthy self-esteem and a positive self-image, I entered my fragile teenage years entirely unprepared for the emotional roller coaster ride that lay ahead.

I had been surrounded by musical talent my entire life. Both my mother and my sister Michele were exceptional pianists, dad's hobby was performing in local musicals, and my sister Marlene played guitar and some piano. My *Zaide* was a retired Orthodox Cantor, well known for his extraordinary voice. *Zaide* had a soulful, spiritual connection that he joyfully expressed through song; he was humming or singing whenever I saw him. Following in my family's footsteps, I played guitar, played the piano by ear, and wrote songs; all starting at the age of six.

Often our family gathered in the living room in the evening after dinner. My father, Marlene, and I loved to sing. The three of us would harmonize while my mother and Michele took turns accompanying us on the piano. We had developed quite a large repertoire of old songs and show tunes.

We looked like the picture perfect, happy family: like we had stepped right out of a Norman Rockwell painting. On Sundays when friends or family visited our home we would entertain them. Everyone seemed to love our shows. Looking back at our hammed-up *shtick* I'm surprised that our guests actually enjoyed the amateur hour. Life was much simpler back then.

Music nurtured my soul; transported me to another realm. My guitar was like another appendage of mine; I spent hours alone in my room each day playing it, singing, and writing songs. I brought my guitar along with me everywhere I went. My friends always wanted me to entertain them; they used to tell me that I'd be famous one day.

With my love of music it was only natural for me to gravitate towards other teenagers with the same focus. At the beginning of tenth grade I met a talented group of kids from my high school and we formed a rock and roll band called Xalice (Weird name? I know...I actually voted against it!). We became a family of sorts and spent all of our free time together. I sang lead vocals with another girl. I also played some acoustic guitar and wrote songs for the band. Determined for our group to become successful, we worked hard, but we always had a great time together. My fondest teenage memories are of those times.

Then in the spring of my fifteenth year I had an unfortunate accident that altered my life as I knew it.

While out with some friends late one weekend night, I accidentally slammed the heavy door of my friend's car on the tip of my left index finger. At first I didn't realize what had happened, but when I looked down to see the damage I realized that part of my finger was missing.

As I screamed in horror, the driver of the car jumped out and came to my aid. He hurriedly grabbed a towel out of his trunk to wrap my gaping, hemorrhaging wound. Fortunately he'd had some paramedic training and knew what to do in an emergency. With his lights flashing and me riding shotgun, still screaming bloody murder, he rushed me to the nearest hospital. A plastic surgeon sutured my wound in the ER but the damage was permanent.

The physical pain of my injury continued to be excruciating for the next two weeks. I was given potent narcotics, but nothing I took even touched the pain. I stayed home and in bed during that time trying to recover from the catastrophe. The physical pain was one thing, but the emotional torment was almost impossible for me to bear. I just couldn't face the fact that I'd be cosmetically scarred for the rest of my life; I'd never be perfect. No one would ever love me again.

When I eventually healed after a few months and the bandage came off, I attempted to play my guitar again. But besides the alteration of my dexterity, it was painful to press down on the strings with that finger. Grievously discouraged, I never played the guitar again.

The entirely exhaustive calamity knocked me into a black hole of depression. I remained inconsolable. I kept saying "why me?" There was nothing anyone could do or say that would help me. I was ruined and that was that.

It would subsequently take me over two decades to emotionally recover from that devastating trauma.

Nine: Just Call Me Boobs

Never be bullied into silence. Never allow yourself to be made a victim. Accept no one's definition of your life, but define yourself.
~ Harvey S. Firestone

My first two years at Milford Mill High School had been tumultuous and overshadowed by depression. My grades were decent, though I hadn't applied myself academically at all. As far as I was concerned I was just biding my time till I could get out of there. Once I reached my senior year I wanted to have as little to do with the school as possible.

The only specific academic requirement for seniors was twelfth grade English. Still the students were required to fill their days with classes for their remaining graduation credits.

The seniors were offered an alternative to spending the entire day at school with a program called D.O., or Diversified Occupation. Enrolling in that program meant taking English and a D.O. class every morning, then working at a paying job outside of the school for the remainder of the day. Enough credits were earned through that program to graduate at the end of the year. Perfect!

At the beginning of the school year I was assigned a job at the office of a company that billed patients for their doctor visits. The three men that owned the company were all part of the same family. Two of the partners were Filipino brothers, both married, and the third one was their sister's American husband. I worked in the downstairs office with another lady and the partners had a separate office upstairs.

The brothers were crude and unscrupulous men. I knew for a fact that one of them had a separate apartment from the one he shared with his pregnant wife; a place that he used to have an affair with another woman. As far as I could see there was nothing wrong with their brother-in-law; he seemed well-mannered and quiet.

The brothers came up with a nickname for me. They never called me by my real name; they just called me "Boobs." With their accents it sounded more like *Bull-bs* (pronounced like a male cow with a BS). I guess at the time I thought my pet-name was humorous and certainly harmless, but I was very wrong.

One afternoon, after having worked in the office for about six months, the brothers called downstairs and asked me to come upstairs to their private office. I'd never gone up there before; I had no idea what they needed me to do. I took the building elevator to the second floor, searched for their suite number, then knocked on their office door. I heard a friendly voice with a recognizable Filipino accent respond, "Come on in, Boobs. The door is unlocked."

I opened the door and saw the two brothers casually swiveling back and forth in their desk chairs, looking at me with stupid smiles on their faces. "Come in, don't be shy," they said, practically in unison. I walked in and closed the door behind me.

They both stood up and guided me through a wide, opened doorway to an adjacent room. The first thing I noticed in that room was the long, yellow upholstered bench that was positioned against the back wall. A large chrome and glass étagère, neatly stacked with a massive collection of magazines, stood against the wall on the left side of the room.

One of them patted his hand on the cushioned bench and said, "Sit here, Boobs."

As I reluctantly lowered myself onto the seat I noticed the other brother removing a magazine from one of the many piles on the étagère. He brought it over to me, opened it to a specific page, and laid it on my lap. The picture he was showing me was of a nude young girl, seductively posed inside a pornographic magazine. "That girl is seventeen just like you. Is that what *you* look like, Boobs?"

Alarmed but not wanting to give them the satisfaction of seeing me squirm, I nonchalantly responded, "I don't think so."

"We think so," one of them quickly retorted. With a cheesy smile on his face he asked, "Why don't you take off your shirt and show us your boobs?"

"Are you kidding? I'm *not* taking off my shirt for you!" I stated with resolve. But they had isolated me and I was concerned. I didn't know what sinister intentions they had planned for me.

Trying to coerce and intimidate me he said, "Are you too modest? Come on Boobs, don't be a chicken!"

"I'm not modest at all but I'm *not* going to take off my shirt," I asserted.

Clearly enjoying the game, they kept the pressure on me for a few minutes longer. Then to my great relief, one of them finally said to the other, "She's too chicken." He turned toward me showing deliberately exaggerated disgust and said, "We're done with you. You can go back downstairs now, Boobs."

I didn't have to be told twice. I hurried back downstairs, finished out the day, and then went home.

When I showed up for work the next morning I was immediately fired.

Though I'd been caught off guard, I have to admit that their despicable behavior did not surprise me. I had come to expect that kind of behavior from grown men. It never occurred to me to report those men for "sexual harassment." In fact the term had yet to be originated. Ironically, the very first sexual harassment court decision in America was actually made that same year, 1976. It wasn't until 1991 that the label "sexual harassment" had become a household expression.

I didn't want to share the details of that degrading experience with anyone. I don't know why but I somehow felt responsible for their actions. Maybe I'd unintentionally sent out a signal that they decided to act on. Embarrassed, I concocted a story to explain the loss of my job to my teacher and my mother. What was the harm? I knew no one would ever find out the truth.

I took my lumps and added the experience to my internal emotional crap pile.

Ten: Read My Lips Sir

Problems are not stop signs,
they're guidelines.
~ Robert Schuller

I graduated high school in June of 1976. That year was especially notable because it was the bicentennial anniversary of our country. Tall, majestic sailing ships from all over the world were docked at Baltimore's newest attraction, The Inner Harbor. Thousands of tourists flooded the city each day. The city was alive with festivities and celebrations the entire summer.

Baltimore was one of the main destination cities for bicentennial celebrations because it holds a great deal of historical relevance to our country. Fort McHenry, best known for defending the Baltimore Harbor in 1812 from the British Army, was a huge tourist draw. Ft. McHenry is where Francis Scott Key wrote our national anthem, *The Star Spangled Banner*.

As the eventful summer came to a close, I switched gears and prepared myself for college, the next chapter of my life. I had chosen to attend a local college, Towson State University, as a commuter, and live at home. The idea of sharing a tiny room with strange girls and sharing a bathroom with dozens of girls did not appeal to me. I didn't think any of the girls would like me anyway; I wasn't the "rah rah" type. I have to admit that my number one reason for staying around was that I didn't want to leave my high-school boyfriend of two years. And since my sisters had already relocated to other states, I felt guilty about abandoning my mother.

Based on my history I should have known better than to continue living with my parents. Before long it was obvious that I had made a very bad decision. Things did not go well at home.

As a commuter I never quite tapped into the excitement of college life. Although I made a few friends on campus I had to find my social life elsewhere. The only places to meet new people were night clubs and bars; not the best places to find quality friendships or decent men. But I didn't care; at eighteen I wanted to be careless, wild, and crazy.

I excitedly began the fall semester at Towson State University with two majors, Art and Psychology. My plan was to eventually merge the two majors into one and graduate as an Art Therapist.

My art and psychology classes were fabulous; I found them interesting and was a natural in those areas. But my lack of focus in high school proved to be detrimental for me in college. I didn't know how to study and my language arts skills were atrocious. I did very well in Art and Psychology, but I barely treaded water in my freshman prerequisite courses. Still, I kept my goal in focus, persevered, and made it through my freshman year.

I had similar issues in the first semester of my sophomore year. I was also frustrated with the amount of out-of-school time I had to devote to my art assignments.

During the second semester of my sophomore year, I took a sculpting class that was required for my major. The greatest percentage of our final grade for that class was based on the completion of a wood sculpture. I came up with an original idea, sketched out a plan for an abstract wall sculpture, and approached the challenge with the utmost enthusiasm.

The technique I used was intricate and time consuming. I started with two-by-four planks of knot-free pine, cut them into several small blocks with a table saw, and then carved each block into a different abstract shape with a jigsaw. Each piece required hand sanding and staining. The next step was to strategically mount them on a flat, wooden surface that had been pre-cut, sanded, and stained. The finished sculpture was an interesting three-dimensional study of depth and shading. I amassed more than a hundred hours of painstaking handiwork. My mother loved the piece so I promised to give it to her after it was graded.

I completed my project just before spring break. My instructor was very impressed with my work and gave me an A-plus. He said that he'd really like to display my sculpture in the Fine Arts building and asked if I'd mind loaning it to him. Although I was anxious to bring my prized piece home, his admiration flattered me enough that I agreed to entrust him with it.

When I returned to school after the break I went to the Fine Arts building, excited to see my piece on display. I searched the gallery and the various display cases throughout the building but I couldn't locate my sculpture. After searching every floor of the building with no luck, I went to the sculpting studio to ask my instructor where he'd displayed it. His answer floored me.

He explained that he'd hung it on a nail on the wall (I already couldn't believe my ears) and over the break someone stole it. *Well of course they did you moron! What did you expect?*

Hoping that someone at school knew its whereabouts, I placed an ad in the university newspaper and posted signs all around campus. No one responded. My prized piece was forever gone.

Not only was I furious; I was heartbroken. That was the second time since I'd injured my finger that I'd poured my soul into creative self-expression and had been thwarted. Roadblocks had been placed in the path of the only two passions that kept me sane; music and art.

Had I been stronger, I could have jumped those minor hurdles. But I wasn't. It took very little to tip me over the edge. My enthusiasm for school disappeared right along with the missing sculpture. After completing my sophomore year of college, I dropped out.

Living at home had become unbearable. My parents despised my new boyfriend, Greg. The things they hated about him were the exact traits that had drawn me to him to begin with; he wasn't Jewish and he was a smart-aleck, bad-boy type. And try as they might, their hostile attempts to dissuade the relationship only backfired; the more they pushed to keep me away from him, the further they drove me into his arms.

They were disgusted with my attitude and disagreed with the choices I was making. I'd had my fill of their redundant lectures and histrionic reactions. Rebellion boiled inside of me then shot out like steam from a tea kettle. I knew I'd better find a job and move out of there before my parents and I killed each other.

I searched the Baltimore Sun's classified ads and before long I found a full-time office-clerk job, working for a company in downtown Baltimore that financed auto insurance premiums. My salary was minimal; I could eke by on my own. But in order to move out of my parents' house I'd have to find a roommate to share expenses with.

After combing the Sun's ads again, and checking out a few unsavory people with their less-than-desirable living conditions, I found a promising ad in the "roommate wanted" section of the Jewish Times (a popular local publication). A female living in a two-bedroom, two-bath apartment was looking for another female to share expenses with. I had a feeling that this one was going to be a good fit.

Sandra and I met and our personalities instantly clicked. I loved her apartment; it was spacious and clean, I liked the location, and best of all I could afford it. I'd found my new home.

Only nineteen years old, I felt very grown up in my independent lifestyle. I liked not having to answer to anyone and didn't mind working hard to pay for that privilege. The only drawback was that my salary didn't afford me much spending money after all the bills were paid. Sandra, a professional with a degree, earned nearly twice the salary that I did.

The experience of working and living on my own had given me a boost of self-confidence. After struggling to support myself for two years, I began to think about finding a more professional job, one that would offer some type of marketable skill-training as well as a larger salary.

I went back to the trusty Sun classifieds again and began job searching.

A prominent downtown Baltimore malpractice law firm had placed a help-wanted ad for an office clerk in the Sunday paper. The ad stated that the position included paralegal training. That sounded perfect for me; exactly what I'd been looking for. I read the ad to make sure that I met all the experiential requirements, and then called first thing Monday morning to set up an interview.

An interview was scheduled with the president of the firm, a powerful, successful malpractice attorney, known for winning several multi-million dollar cases. I really wanted that job; I knew it could turn my life around. My plan was to walk in his office brimming with confidence, give the man a firm handshake, and proceed to knock his socks off.

That's exactly what I did and it worked like a charm. Though the attorney had presented himself pompously and was slightly condescending, it did appear that I'd impressed him. I must have done something right because I walked out of the interview with the job.

The starting salary for the position was slightly more than my current income, enough to loosen up my finances, but the paralegal training would secure my future. The next morning I gave a two week notice to my employer that I would be leaving my job.

On the first morning of my new employment, excited to embark on my new career, I reported directly to the executive secretary to get my instructions. She seemed a bit caught off guard; it appeared that no one had briefed her on my duties yet. Not knowing what she was supposed to do with me, she sat me at an empty desk and suggested that I read magazines until further notice. By the day's end there still was no "further notice."

She wasn't any more prepared for me the second morning when I reported to her, so again she suggested I continue to read magazines until further notice. She did however add one responsibility to my nonexistent work load; she gave me specific instructions on the proper way to answer the telephone. Her instructions were as follows:

1. Never put any calls through to the attorneys.
2. Always say, "Mr. So and So is in a meeting, may I take a message?"

She also emphasized that the president of the firm, the man I'd interviewed with, must always be addressed as "Sir."

Every morning for the next four days, I'd show up at work and report to the secretary. And each morning she'd tell me the exact same thing; read magazines and answer the telephone until further notice.

After thirty-two hours of doing little else but twiddling my thumbs (I'd already read every magazine in the entire firm), I began to get antsy. I interrogated the secretary who frigidly suggested that I be patient. *Gee thanks!*

Finally when Friday rolled around, the snooty secretary advised me that "Sir" had instructed her to begin my training first thing Monday morning.

I arrived at work the following Monday morning, excited to finally start learning my new job. As was required, I reported directly to the executive secretary. She instructed me to get my coat; we were going on an errand.

The secretary led me out into the hall and down an elevator to an underground garage. She pointed to the fleet of company cars parked in a row in the basement of the building, as we approached them. In a very business-like manner she explained that we would be driving to Washington D.C. to pick up "Sir's" weekly wholesale produce order. She handed me a legal pad and recommended that I take notes since I would eventually assume that responsibility on my own. *What a peculiar responsibility,* I thought to myself.

She drove the car. I rode next to her in the passenger seat and wrote down the directions on my legal pad as had been instructed. When we arrived at the wholesale market an hour later, the secretary showed me how to inspect the produce order to make sure it was fresh and accurate, and then the two of us loaded the ridiculously large glut of boxes containing fruits and vegetables into the back of the company station wagon. Since she had already explained to me that "Sir" lived alone with his disabled wife, I couldn't imagine what he planned to do with all that perishable food.

We left the market and headed back to Baltimore. I continued to take notes on my legal pad.

Our first stop in Baltimore was at the Dry Cleaners to pick up "Sir's" clothes. After that, the secretary drove to his house to drop off his dry cleaning and to transfer the boxes of produce from the back of the station wagon into his garage. When everything was done, we headed back downtown to the office.

The next morning, and every morning for the remainder of the week, I was ignored again. My only option was to restlessly revert back to thumb twiddling for eight hours a day, though I did make an interesting observation as I sat there. "Sir" apparently had a woman-friend (wink, wink) who also "worked" at the office. I guess his poor, disabled wife at home couldn't satisfy him enough.

Anyway, another Monday rolled around and I received word from the executive secretary in the morning that "Sir" wanted to see me in his private office.

I entered his office, he asked me to take a seat, and then offered me a soda from his personal refrigerator. He apologized for ignoring me but said that he'd been trying to decide where to place me. Then "Sir" began elaborating on a job that did not resemble the one I'd been hired for in any way. He explained that the job he was offering me was one of great responsibility. I would be, to use his words, his "right-hand assistant." He told me that he would provide me with a beeper so that he could reach me twenty-four/seven. He said that the choice was mine; I could still have the job that he'd originally hired me for if I preferred.

Though I was unprepared for his new proposal, I was aware of his cunning, manipulative capabilities. The second option immediately sent up red flags in my mind. I was leery of accepting that kind of job proposal from him, especially with that amount of commitment. I told him that I'd feel more comfortable with the first job option.

Appearing satisfied with my decision, "Sir" said that was fine.

When I came to work the following morning, the Tuesday of my third week, a partner I hadn't yet met asked me to come into his office. I figured that he was going to give me some work to do for him. He offered me a seat in his office, closed the door behind him, and then sat down at his desk to face me. I saw him look directly at me and then slightly drop his eyes. "You're fired," he said as gently as possible under the circumstances.

My jaw dropped. "I haven't even started the job yet! What did I do?" I asked him, stunned.

"You answered the question wrong," he replied, nodding at me in a knowing way.

I'd been set up...and there was nothing I could do about it.

If only I could have fast-forwarded into the future I probably wouldn't have felt as bad as I did. It's funny how things happen in life. As the saying goes, "What goes around comes around."

Ten years later, two federal agents tracked me down and popped in to see me at my job. They said that they had some questions to ask me, so I invited them to take a seat in my office. They asked me if I had worked at "Sir's" law firm back in 1979 and asked me to explain the circumstances of my termination. I was happy to share my story, though still unsure of why they had come to see me.

They explained that "Sir" was under criminal investigation for repeated sexual harassment of his female employees. Apparently over the years, "Sir" had habitually hired young blonde-haired women who looked just like me, then fired them in the same exact manner. Based on my history, that didn't surprise me at all. But it did make me giddily happy to know that he'd been reported. The score was about to be settled and I sold him right down the river! I felt so empowered.

Eleven: Violated

The gem cannot be polished without friction nor man without trials.
~ *Confuscius*

Jobless through no fault of my own, unemployment compensation was the only immediate solution to my financial concerns. I needed that income to pay my bills until I found another job.

After two months of searching, I found a full-time position as the credit manager of a popular jewelry store in the Reisterstown Road Plaza. The job worked out well for me; I was given full charge of the credit department and could basically run my own show. It was refreshing not to have to cow-tow to anyone.

While commuting to work from my apartment one morning, I accidentally rear-ended another car at a traffic light. Since no speed was involved, just the split-second, accidental stepping of my foot on the gas pedal, no one suffered any injuries. And though the other car showed barely a dent, the front end of my car folded up like a crushed soda can.

After assessing the damage to my car, due to its age, the insurance company considered it a total loss. I eventually received a settlement check for two thousand dollars. I'd never been able to accumulate a nest egg due to my limited income, so I deposited the settlement check in the bank for a rainy day.

Luckily my parents were planning to buy a new car so they gave me their 1969 avocado-green Pontiac Lemans. I was immensely grateful for the gift.

At this point I'd been living with Sandra for over two years. Our roommate arrangement was working out well; we had become close friends and enjoyed sharing the apartment together.

She had recently started dating Bob, a guy that lived on the first floor of our apartment building. We lived on the second floor. Bob seemed to be a nice, hardworking, stable guy. As Sandra and Bob's relationship grew stronger, she began spending more and more time with him and often slept downstairs at his apartment.

Greg (the boyfriend that my parents despised) and I had been seeing each other for two years. The basis of our entire relationship was drama and heart-ache. As long as I'd known Greg, his life had been chronically problematic; a compounded list of troubles, legal and otherwise, trailed him like Pigpen's cloud of dirt and dust.

Though I found our relationship frustrating and arduous, his brilliant mind and charismatic personality held me captive. I found him curiously interesting, mysterious, and deeply pensive; he wrote volumes of poetry for and about me. I could never understand why, but he never seemed to fulfill the tremendous potential that I saw in him.

Greg and I were both down and out but in very different ways. Greg was a "grifter" who would con or flimflam anybody he could to get by. He could best be described as sketchy; I never knew what he was up to. On the other side of the coin, I was a good-hearted, honest person who just had a depleted spirit.

It took two years of pandemonium for me to reach my saturation point with Greg. Once I began receiving threatening telephone calls from the wrathful scoundrels he had double-crossed, I decided that I'd had enough. I finally saw the light and booted his shifty ass right out of my life.

I thought I'd feel relieved to rid my life of all the tumult, but I have to admit...I felt worse. Not only was I painfully lonely without Greg, but I was bored out of my mind. I thought I wanted normalcy though I continued to fill the chaotic void with more chaos.

At the time I hadn't a clue as to why my life was so helter-skelter, but I understand now. After having been bombarded by drama and pain in some way, shape, or form since childhood, I thrived on its negative energy. I was addicted to it. I did not know how to exist without it.

I'd only experienced the lull for a month or two when bedlam came knocking at my door. Just a few weeks shy of my twenty-second birthday I came face-to-face with a terrifying, living-nightmare.

On Monday night, August 25, 1980 I went to sleep alone in my apartment; Sandra was spending the night downstairs at Bob's place. Around three a.m. in the morning a strange mixture of sounds woke me out of my sleep. I heard the squishing sound that the padding under my carpet made whenever it was stepped on, and my Cockatiel, Civet, was hissing wildly from his cage near my bedroom door. Civet was a mean bird who hissed anytime someone came near his cage. My heart began pounding with terror; I knew there was an intruder in my room.

I opened my eyes, but all I could see without my glasses on was a tall dark figure standing by Civet's cage. I'd closed my bedroom door before going to sleep and now I could see the bathroom nightlight shining in from the hallway. Praying to God that it was someone I knew I called out, "Who's there?"

Suddenly a knife was at my throat. A man that spoke with an African-American dialect put his mouth against my right ear and ordered "Don't move!" I immediately closed my eyes. He pressed the knife harder against my neck while he climbed on top of my body to pin me down. Screaming would have been futile and most likely fatal because no one would have heard me.

He asked me where my mother was. I had no idea what he was talking about so I didn't answer.

As he forced his weight upon my torso, I felt the clammy sweat from his shirtless chest transferring to my skin. He seemed much taller and stronger than I was and he reeked of cherry-scented oil. A dangling necklace of some sort, which rattled as he moved, hung from his neck. With no time to act and no chance of escape, my mind scrambled for a survival strategy.

I kept my eyes shut tight; if I lived, I didn't want that tormenting vision haunting me forever. Breathless from panic, and trembling, I asked him to please put the knife down.

"You'd better calm down!" he nervously demanded.

Between terrified, breathless sobs, I insisted that I couldn't calm down. I told him that he could do whatever he wanted to me and I'd cooperate, but I couldn't possibly cooperate with a knife against my throat. My second survival strategy was telling him that I'd keep a pillow over my face so he'd know I couldn't identify him afterwards.

To my surprise and relief he heeded to my desperate plea. He moved the knife away from my throat and then reached over and laid it down on my dresser.

I tried to catch my breath and compose myself as much as possible. The only other survival tool I had readily at my disposal was my well-practiced ability to reason with unreasonable people and calm them down. In order to regain some control I'd have to employ psychological tactics and hope that he possessed a shred of moral fiber. If I could connect with his conscience and gain his compassion I knew that I stood a chance.

I thanked him for putting the knife down. With a pillow over my face and keeping my tone friendly, I asked him why he had chosen me.

"I saw you sitting outside on the front steps of your building, talking to your mother," he began to explain. I knew who he was referring to; she was my next-door neighbor, not my mother.

"I wanted you. I knew I could never be with you, but I just had to have you," he continued. *Oh wonderful...here we go again. Why was I always a creep magnet?*

I thanked him for his flattery and strategically quipped, "Why did you go to all this trouble to be with me when you could have just asked me out? I probably would have said yes!"

He continued without reacting to my comment, "I used the picnic table from your neighbor's patio below your balcony to climb on. I pulled myself up and over the railing and climbed onto your balcony. Then I shook your sliding glass door until it opened and walked into your living room." He seemed proud to share his accomplishment. I'd been wondering, but now I understood how he'd gotten past the deadbolt lock on our front door.

He'd been stalking me. Not only had he been watching me from the front of my building, he'd been surveying the back too. Our apartment faced the woods in the back of the building. He knew that no one would hear him or see what he was intending on doing in the pitch-black darkness of the night. The calculation of his plan made my blood run cold.

He'd begun to let his guard down and seemed willing to talk. With the pillow still covering my face I began asking him questions about what I hoped was the closest thing to his heart...his mother. If that couldn't soften him up, nothing could. I also asked him if he currently or ever had a girlfriend. He told me that he'd had girlfriends in the past but didn't have one at the time.

Reaching in as deep into his mind as I possibly could, I asked him, "How would you feel if a man violated your mother or a woman you loved like you were violating me?"

He actually thought for a second then said, "I'd be enraged."

Based on his responses I made the quick assumption that he wasn't a maniacal sociopath. That gave me hope that I might survive the night, though I knew the possibility still remained that he'd panic at some point and decide to kill me. At any rate, I had bought myself some time.

I began to sense that somewhere in his deranged mind he had developed feelings for me. He assured me that as long as I stayed calm and cooperated with him, he'd do what he came to do then leave. And in a warped attempt to show me some consideration he claimed he wouldn't ejaculate inside of me. That turned out to be a lie. Clearly I had no say in any of his decisions so I blocked out my mind and gritted my teeth underneath my pillow as he proceeded to rape me.

When he completed the act he told me that he was going to leave; he said that he would throw a rock at my window to let me know that he had safely escaped so I could call for help. I listened for the rock but never heard his signal.

Paralyzed with fear, unsure of his whereabouts, I lay in my bed trembling. I listened for sounds but heard only silence. With an unsteady hand I reached over to my nightstand, grabbed the telephone receiver, and dialed Bob's telephone number downstairs.

It was four o'clock in the morning; Bob answered the phone sounding half asleep. He heard my voice and immediately handed the receiver to Barbara.

I began hysterically ranting.

"He raped me! Oh my God...he broke in and he raped me! He came in my room...I was sleeping. Oh God, please help me!"

Stunned, she asked, "Are you okay? Who raped you? What happened?"

"Call the police and tell them to hurry!" I demanded. "Please help me!"

Sandra listened in utter disbelief. "I'll call 911, then I'll be right there!" she assured me.

I hung up the telephone. Then forcing my trembling legs to stand up, I cautiously tiptoed to the doorway of my room. Still listening for sounds I peered left and right down the hallway; the coast seemed clear. I ran directly from my room to the living room to relock the sliding glass doors. The front door had remained dead bolted; he'd left the same way he'd come in.

As I had hurried past the kitchen on my way into the living room I'd noticed an open drawer, so I backtracked to investigate. The drawer he'd left open was where we kept our cutlery. It appeared that he'd rummaged through the drawer and selected the knife that he'd held against my throat. Then I turned left out of the kitchen and walked down to the end of the hall where Sandra's bedroom was. As I entered her room the words "Oh my God" burst out of my hand-covered mouth. The wire leading to her telephone lay on the floor, sliced in half.

Suddenly the entire picture came together in my mind. I thought about him asking me where my mother was, watching me outside with the woman next door, and then seeing Sandra's antique bedroom furnishings. He thought that Sandra's room was my mother's room. If she hadn't slept down-stairs that night she would have become his first vic-tim.

When Sandra came upstairs, she looked around and discovered that the wires to the living room and kitchen telephones had been sliced in half too. Just imagining the possibilities of his original plan and tracing his surreptitious steps made the crime feel that much more menacing. As far I as was con-cerned, it didn't matter if they ever caught the rapist, I was grateful to have survived the night.

The police arrived within a few minutes. Two detectives showed up with the officers. While one detective went around the apartment dusting for fingerprints, the other one asked me to show him the crime scene. He followed me to my bedroom. The detective put latex gloves on then carefully bagged my bed sheets and my nightgown to keep as evidence.

After they took my victim's statement, they transported me by squad car to the Baltimore Coun-ty Rape Crisis Center at the Greater Baltimore Medi-cal Center. A forensic gynecologist examined me us-ing a "rape kit" to gather fluids and hair samples. To prevent pregnancy I was given a "morning after pill." I couldn't believe that this was all happening to me. The entire event seemed surreal.

DNA profiling did not exist in 1980. With all the evidence gathered, the detectives would still need me to positively identify the perpetrator. But that was impossible; I never saw his face. The detectives visited me twice at my apartment to show me mug shots but I couldn't help at all. I consoled myself with the fact that my prayers had been answered. I had survived the attack alive and physically uninjured. I was immensely grateful. I didn't feel entitled to ask for anything more than my life.

In the weeks and months following the incident, I came to realize how emotionally detached from the rape I was feeling. Besides the residual fear from the violence of the crime, I saw the violation as yet another man using me for his own gratification. Sadly to say, I'd probably become desensitized long before the rape even occurred. I never went for counseling afterwards because I didn't believe I needed it.

The friendship between Sandra and I rapidly deteriorated after the rape. I was belligerent, selfish and rude; I became the roommate from hell. When Greg found out what had happened to me, he bought me a Shetland Sheepdog puppy for protection that I named Shane. But Shane wasn't housebroken, the entire apartment began to reek of urine, and he chewed on everything. Sandra was furious.

The tension between us grew more and more unbearable by the day. In a rage I moved out while Sandra was at work one day. My name wasn't on the lease so she was left with all the expenses. She did not deserve that treatment but I couldn't have cared less at the time. I had become a complete trainwreck; I just didn't know it.

Shane and I moved into an efficiency apartment in a high-rise building nearby. The building could only be entered with a special resident's card. That gave me some sense of security. Frightened and lonely, in need of comfort and familiarity, I unwisely allowed Greg back into my life.

At twenty-two, the emotional walls I'd built for protection as a child now functioned only two ways, completely up or completely down. Either I shut off my feelings entirely or indiscriminately opened myself up. When my walls were down, I was basically a sitting duck.

Greg knew everything about me. No one knew my state of mind better than he did. He knew that financially I was just making ends meet, and he also knew about the two thousand dollar settlement I'd squirreled away in the bank, because we were together during that time. As a solution to my financial problems he suggested a "sure-fire" scheme to double my money.

The plan had something to do with buying and selling gold; it sounded blatantly suspicious just like every other scheme he'd ever hatched. I wasn't willing to risk my measly financial cushion on a shell game. When he insisted that I entrust him with my money for a few hours so he could double the amount, I was understandably reluctant.

Greg worked me over for days, hurt and insulted that I wouldn't allow him to help me. He made me feel guilty for not trusting him; he reminded me that in the two years I'd known him he'd never stolen anything from me. Greg finally succeeded in wearing me down, but I told him that I was only willing to risk half my money, only one thousand dollars. He swore on his life that he would never rip me off.

I withdrew one thousand dollars from the bank, handed it over to him, and off he went to make the deal.

True to his word and to my great relief he returned to me the same day with two thousand-dollars in his hand. I didn't know how he pulled it off but it was very convincing.

Assured that he'd gained my confidence, he asked me to give him the entire three thousand-dollars and he'd return with six thousand-dollars in a few hours. He insisted that he was sure he could triple my original amount. But that being all the money I had to my name, it wasn't a risk I was willing to take

He worked me over again for a few more days. After his unrelenting pressuring and against my better judgment I finally gave in and withdrew the rest of the cash from the bank.

He left with my money... but he didn't return so soon.

I worried as the clock ticked away the hours. My panic level escalated as the hours turned into days, weeks, and then months. He seemed to vanish into thin air, leaving my impoverished spirit and my empty bank account behind. I never heard from or saw him again.

I know it appears that I made a stupid mistake and ultimately got what I deserved. I'm the last one to make excuses, but he clearly capitalized on my vulnerability when I was at my lowest. It took me a few years but I finally put two and two together and realized that Greg had been a junkie; drug addiction had been pulling his strings and driving his desperation. That explained a lot.

The back-to-back violations had left me feeling worthless and powerless. Depression sapped my energy and my motivation. I lacked the emotional fortitude needed to pull myself up by the bootstraps.

But one thing I never lost was my ability to dream. I clung to the fairytale-like hope that someday my knight in shining armor would arrive on his white horse, sweep me off my feet, and carry me off into the sunset. Then everything that was ever wrong would be right again.

Twelve: The Tarnished White Knight

Life is like a game of cards. The hand you're dealt is determinism; the way you play it is free will.
~ Jawaharlal Nehru

L ike many single young-women in the early eighties, my girlfriends and I enjoyed getting all dolled-up on the weekends and going out to discotheques. We hoped to meet nice guys to date; though the guys that frequented the discos were usually alcoholics, drug addicts, or narcissistic losers. When we'd get there we'd loosen up with mixed drinks then dance all night to the music.

A new discotheque called Christopher's had recently opened in Baltimore. The club booked the hottest local bands on the weekends, gaining them instant popularity with the single crowd. Well-dressed "twenty-somethings" packed the dance floor every night.

My girlfriend Debbie and I were hanging out at Christopher's one night when a group of guys a few years older than us that we'd known from high school walked in. I didn't recall ever having seen them there before that night; they didn't seem like the typical kind of guys that would go to a place like that. Debbie and I said hello to them, then I walked away to use the ladies room. Debbie stayed there and continued to talk with them.

I guess I wasn't paying very close attention. Out of the five or six guys from their group that we talked to that night, I may have remembered seeing three or four that I recognized. After I came out of the ladies room, I began talking to someone else.

The guys didn't hang around very long, though I hadn't noticed that they'd left until Debbie came looking for me. She said that one of the guys was interested in me and asked her who I was. He also asked her to write my telephone number down on a napkin for him. She told me his name but I'd never heard of him; I didn't notice him standing there with his friends either. I thought it was adorable that he'd been too shy to talk to me. Debbie insisted that I knew who he was.

Every year the junior class of Milford Mill High School would put on a show for the graduating seniors that they'd perform at the senior farewell assembly. Each junior classman portrayed one senior classman, mimicking them and over-emphasizing their idiosyncrasies. Trying to jar my memory Debbie asked, "Remember the part I played in the Milford Mill High School senior farewell play?"

"Yes, and I stood next to you on stage," I recalled. I clearly remembered her part, even though I couldn't remember my own.

"Keith is *so* cute. Keith is *so* wonderful. Keith is *so* rich!" she said re-enacting her role as Keith's prior girlfriend Lauren, using the same obnoxious tone as she had used in the play. "That's him. That's the same Keith!"

I remembered Lauren from high-school but I never knew anything about her boyfriend Keith.

I found the mystery of who Keith was very intriguing. I was anxious for my secret admirer to call me. Debbie thought she had written down the right telephone number, but she wasn't entirely sure since my number was new and she didn't know it very well. After a week went by without hearing from him I began to wonder whether he had changed his mind or just had the wrong phone number.

I couldn't get the thought of Keith out of my head. I can't explain why but I felt like I already knew him and that he was supposed to be in my life.

A few weeks later my graduating class, the Milford Mill High School class of 1976, had their five-year reunion. Even though I never liked school I thought it would be fun to catch up with some friends I'd lost touch with. Debbie and I went to the reunion together.

As the party came to a close I was talking to an old friend of mine and I asked him if he knew of anything else that was happening after the reunion. I figured he'd know about that kind of thing since he had stayed in contact with many people from school. He said that he knew of one party; it was at the house of his older brother's friend.

I knew his brother. In fact he was one of the guys in the group that Debbie and I had seen at Christopher's. I asked him which one of his brother's friends was having the party and he said Keith. I almost fell over.

I couldn't contain my excitement! I told Debbie about the party and she agreed that we should go check it out. By the end of the night I hoped to find out who Keith was, what he looked like, and why he had never called me.

When we arrived at the party, people were overflowing onto the street outside the house. The door to the tall, wooden privacy fence surrounding the backyard stood open. I could see a large, rectangular, in-ground swimming pool as I peered in. A crowd of lively partiers filled the yard. A few rowdy guys kept doing cannonballs off the diving board, devilishly splashing everybody within range. I could see people milling around inside the house too. The minute Debbie and I walked through the gate someone recognized me, grabbed me by the arm, and said, "I can't believe you're here. Come with me, I've got to find Keith!"

I walked up the back steps of the house and waited inside the kitchen, anxious to meet my mystery man. Minutes later an adorable guy came walking toward me. He had a precious face and the sweetest brown eyes I'd ever seen. His face beamed as he smiled from ear to ear. He hugged me tight and said, "I can't believe you showed up to your party!" I looked at him, puzzled. He explained, "After your friend gave me your number I planned this party thinking you'd be my date. But the phone number your friend gave me must have been wrong. Since that night I've asked everyone I could think of but nobody knew how to get in touch with you."

He ran and grabbed a pen. "Tell me your number. I promise I'll write it permanently on my hand so I'll never ever lose it!" He wrote the number in blue ink on the palm of his hand and said he'd definitely call me the next day. I said that I had to go because I was with my girlfriend. We hugged each other and he kissed me gently on my cheek. I found Debbie in the crowd and we left.

Keith seemed too good to be true. I couldn't wait to find out more about him. I think I floated all the way home.

The next evening around eight o'clock my telephone rang. I picked up the phone, said hello, and then a tender voice on the other end softly responded, "Hi Baby." I thought I would melt into a puddle on the floor. He said he was sorry for not calling earlier but his friend had been rushed to the hospital that day; he'd just come back from visiting him. Keith asked when he could see me, if tomorrow evening would be okay. I told him that sounded great.

He'd already planned out our date. He would pick me up around six o'clock in the evening, bring me back to his house, and cook dinner for us. "There are some things you need to know about me, and I want to be the first to tell you. I'll pick you up tomorrow at six. I can't wait to see you. Sleep well baby."

I hung up the phone and stretched out on the sofa, intoxicated by that dreamy conversation. I just wanted to lie there forever and bask in the feeling. I couldn't help but wonder if he was the knight in shining armor that I'd been dreaming about.

My date arrived at my apartment building at six o'clock sharp the next evening. He pressed the code on the keypad outside and I buzzed him in. He showed up at my door in faded blue jeans and a brown collared jersey-knit shirt. I grabbed my purse and we headed toward the elevator down the hall.

Keith had parked his pale yellow Lincoln Continental right outside the front door of the building. *Very impressive,* I noted in my mind.

He lived only about two miles from my apartment building, just a five-minute ride. His house stood on the corner of Cliffedge Road and Judy Lane in a hilly community called Silver Creek. It was a quiet, well-established neighborhood lined with an assortment of modest brick and shingled homes. His house was a traditional brick Cape Cod.

Two separate sets of concrete steps connected by a short walkway led up a hill from the sidewalk to a small, awning-covered porch. The front lawn had apparently been neglected. The evergreen trees were overgrown and their old knobby roots had replaced most of the grass. There was no landscaping to speak of, the dirt beds up against the house were hardened and cracked. A white magnolia tree livened up the property a bit with its large showy blooms.

When we entered the house I could immediately see that it needed a woman's touch. The first thing I noticed was the dated gold-marbled mirror squares covering one wall of the small living room. The brownish-tan carpet throughout the first floor looked stained and worn. An ugly brown velour sofa faced the mirrored wall.

Keith gave me the usual first-visit house tour. He explained that he had grown up in that house. His parents, who he claimed "used to be poor," had lived there while raising him and his brother. *That explained the tacky, marbled mirrored wall,* I thought to myself. He'd purchased the house from his parents when he married his ex-wife Lauren, the girl I'd know from school. By then his parents had become very successful and had moved to a nicer home. It became more and more obvious that very little had changed since they had moved out of that house.

Steep steps starting just inside the front door led upstairs to two windowed dormer rooms anchoring each side of the house. The pitched ceilings in both of the dormers were coated with glossy black paint and the walls and floors of those claustrophobic rooms were covered in shag carpeting. A beige-pink tiled bathroom was located in the hallway between the two rooms at the top of the stairway.

Back downstairs, a short hallway led from the living room to another bedroom. There had originally been two inadequately sized rooms at the end of the hall, but the wall between them had been removed, creating one long, rectangular room. A king-sized bed over-filled the narrow width on the right side, leaving the left side of the room with a hodge-podge of unrelated furnishings. The closet doors were missing, revealing stereo equipment sitting on top of a recessed old dresser and a record album collection that stood upright inside of built-in wooden cubbyholes.

A door in the middle of the first floor hallway marked the way downstairs to the basement. At the bottom of the unfinished wooden stairway, the front room was paneled in knotty pine and the floor was covered in rust-orange colored shag carpeting. The room featured a large matching knotty pine built-in bar, fully stocked, clearly a remnant of his parents' ownership.

The left side of the basement remained unfinished with dismal gray cinder-block walls and a stained concrete slab floor. An open French drain edged the entire perimeter of the room. An array of unrelated paraphernalia, such as a life-sized Santa-Claus doll, an old electric, vibrating chin/neck firmer, and an open cardboard box filled to the top with baseball cards were piled haphazardly on folding banquet tables. Non-essential clothing that his parents had left when they'd moved out hung on rods suspended by chains from the wood studded ceiling. A dangling light bulb socket with a pull chain and two small casement windows afforded mediocre lighting. One corner with a clothes washer, dryer, and utility sink, designated the laundry room area.

The linoleum floored kitchen/dining room area was located upstairs in the back half of the first floor through a different doorway on the right side of the living room. The tiny kitchen that had never been updated still had the original, twenty-five year old white metal cabinets. A rectangular, almond colored table cluttered the dining room area with its six matching chairs. The kitchen door led outside to the backyard/ pool area.

Apparently he had concentrated all his energies on beautifying the country club style backyard, by far the best feature of the entire house. The yard had been cemented over and covered in bright green Astroturf. A well-tended landscaping bed next to the tall wooden privacy fence surrounded the yard. A

small bathhouse filled wall to wall with pool acces-
sories stood off to the left side of the yard strategically obscuring the pool pump behind it. Vibrant red
begonias and ivy vines spilled over the sides of two
planters, and a basket of brightly colored impatiens
hung from the arm of a white, ornamental light post.
A spacious in-ground swimming pool spanned almost the entire width of the property with three
wide steps across the right side and a diving board
on the other end. Lounge chairs were scattered
around.

A graying old black cat lazily wandered around
the backyard. Keith picked up the cat and brought
him over to me. "I'd like you to meet Leon," he said
as he gently stroked the cat's fur.

"Well hello Leon, nice to meet you." I reached
out and pet the cat's head.

"Do you want to know why I named him
Leon?" Keith asked me, grinning.

"I was wondering. That's a really funny name
for a cat," I answered, grinning back at him.

"He was my friend's cat, but she was moving
and needed to find him a new home. I said that I
would take him. Come on Leon, smile," he said,
laughing. He gently opened the cat's mouth. "I
named him after the boxer Leon Spinks because
they're both missing their front teeth. See?"

I could clearly see the gap between the cat's
teeth. I started giggling. "That's hilarious! What a
perfect name!"

He put Leon back down on the ground and the
cat scampered off.

It was early evening but the sun still shone brightly in the sky. The air was warm with a perfect balmy breeze. Our table for two had already been set poolside. Keith prepared a delicious meal complete with salad, grilled swordfish, and corn on the cob. The atmosphere could not have been more perfect for a first date.

There was so much he wanted to share with me. He said that when he first saw me at Christopher's he said to his friends, "See that girl, I'm going to marry her." Though his statement sounded bizarre at the time, he said he knew we were meant to be together. His confirmation came when I appeared at his house after my high school reunion. We agreed that the fatalistic component of our meeting was undeniable.

"Do you like baseball?" he asked.

I explained that I grew up in a household where four women ruled the roost. Even if my father had wanted to he could never watch sports. Besides everyone in my family was artistically inclined and athletically challenged. I had been to a baseball game or two with friends but I never really got into any sport.

He said, "I'm going to take you to all the Oriole games with me. You'll love baseball."

He gently touched my blonde hair and thoughtfully remarked, "I have a dream. One day I'm going to have a little blonde haired daughter and I'm going to name her Cammy. I'll take her along with me when I go to the Oriole games and I'll hold her little hand while we walk down the stadium steps to our seats. We'll wear matching baseball caps. She'll look so cute in her little hat." I was so moved by his tenderness.

Then he explained the reason for our private first date. "I can't stop thinking about you and I want you in my life more than you could ever imagine. I brought you here so I could explain a part of my past that you probably aren't aware of. Before we go any further, I owe it to you to be honest." I couldn't imagine what he had to tell me.

He continued, "I admitted myself into the Sheppard Pratt Hospital drug rehab program a year ago. I'd lost control of my life and desperately needed help. I spent one month as an inpatient, detoxing and learning how to overcome my heroin addiction. I am now in recovery." He showed me all the track marks up and down his arms. I could not wrap my mind around his admission; he didn't fit the profile. Heroin addicts were not hard working, intelligent suburban homeowners or adorable guys with great personalities and everything going for them. They were destitute bums stumbling around or passed out cold on the sidewalk somewhere. I tried to picture him as a hard-core addict but I just couldn't see it.

The first thing I asked him was if he would ever use again. He responded the way I've since learned that all recovering addicts involved in twelve-step programs respond: "I'm not using today. I take it one day at a time." He couldn't honestly promise me more than that.

I have to admit that his answer devastated me though I didn't let on. I wanted him to tell me that he was cured, to assure me that his drug problem was forever in the past. I wanted him to say that he would never use drugs again. But he couldn't say those words.

I didn't want to have to decide my future right then and there, whether to chance it or walk away. I had no experience, no realistic point of reference in regard to heroin addiction. All I knew was that I didn't want to let this seemingly wonderful guy go, that I had so much more to gain than to lose. He was my Mr. Right, my knight in shining armor. It was all meant to be. This story had to have a happy ending. It just had to.

Thirteen: In the Beginning

Nobody's family can hang out the sign, "Nothing the matter here."
~ *Chinese Proverb*

Wh_en I first met Keith, his older brother Mike was locked up in the state penitentiary for drug related crimes. Mike had a history of previous incarcerations though I don't know how many. What little Keith told me about his brother horrified me. I did not want to meet him. From what I could gather Mike was an evil, cunning creep with a terrible reputation; the kind of guy who'd sell out his best friend for a nickel.

The two brothers were polar opposites. As a child Keith had been sweet and sensitive with a smile that could light up a room. His lovable personality drew people to him. Mike resented him for that.

Their actively social parents often left Mike, five years older, at home to baby-sit for Keith. Jealous over others' adoration of his younger brother, Mike would systematically employ strategies to tarnish Keith's image. He was as adept at hoodwinking his parents as they were blind to the problem.

One night when their parents were out, Keith's brother invited a few of his equally menacing friends over. With Mike acting as the ring leader, the older boys planned a surprise attack on Keith that they thought would be funny. They pounced on him, pinned his arms, and watched him helplessly struggle while Mike injected heroin into his vein. Keith was only fourteen.

Keith's entire life changed that night. Before long, Mike succeeded in getting him addicted to shooting heroin. Unaware of the underlying problem, Keith's parents couldn't control his burgeoning unruly behavior. Keith dropped out of high school at age sixteen and went to work at his father's produce market. Things continued to get worse.

Keith's first love was the needle. As his addiction progressed he added pills like Quaaludes, Dilaudid, Valium, and any other "downs" he could get a hold of. He'd take handfuls at a time. While driving under the influence, he wrecked car after car that his father kept replacing. During one of the accidents Keith broke his jaw. Wired shut for two months he could only eat through a straw; all his meals had to be made in the blender. He laughed reminiscing to me about his "famous" broccoli milkshakes. *Yech!*

He met his ex-wife Lauren sometime between 1974 and 1975. She liked that he was rich; she thought she'd won the lottery. In reality Keith had no money to speak of; it all belonged to his parents. But Lauren hooked her talons into him with no intention of letting go. They had a troubled, drug induced relationship based on co-addiction and drama, not love.

One weekend the two of them went on a gambling trip to Las Vegas and brought along a cache of drugs. The first night of the trip, Lauren doled out the Quaaludes, seeing to it that she gave Keith more than she planned to take herself. Once he was "trashed" and incoherent Lauren dragged him off to a quickie-mart, wedding chapel. Keith woke up the next morning with a wedding ring on his finger and without any recollection of how it had gotten there.

Keith and Lauren had already lived together for two years but he wouldn't have married her otherwise and she knew it. After the Las Vegas trip he figured that as long as they were already married he'd try to make it work. On June 9, 1978 they went to settlement for the Cliffedge Road house as co-owners. Her plan had succeeded; Lauren was as legally tied to Keith as she could possibly get.

But their marriage was a predictable disaster. Things got ugly; they provoked each other constantly and fought over everything. Sometimes their arguments turned into physical fights. In less than one year, their tempestuous marriage was over. And because Lauren owned half of the Cliffedge Road house, Keith was forced to pay her off in the divorce settlement. On September 20, 1979 he became the sole owner of the property, forever free of her.

Fourteen: Getting to Know You

There are two mistakes one can make along the road to truth – Not going all the way, and not starting.
~ Buddha

Nothing seems insurmountable when two people are intoxicated with the feeling of falling in love. Without the conscious recollection of losing each other it seemed Keith and I had found each other again; we were inseparable. Our relationship hit the ground running after our first date, and a few weeks later Shane and I moved into the Cliffedge Road house with Keith and Leon.

Keith had lots of friends and many interests. Life with him was entertaining and refreshing. He enjoyed playing his favorite record albums for me. Among his large, diversified collection was every Rolling Stones album ever recorded; he knew the words to all the songs which he sang with the confidence but definitely not the talent of a virtuoso. And he did a comical impression of Mick Jagger's boastful strut. It was hard to watch his ridiculous antics without bursting into laughter. Keith did a hilarious though not very good impression of Elvis too. He loved listening to Elvis Presley's music and reading books about his life. He knew the words to every song Barbra Streisand had ever recorded. He had a terrible voice but he didn't care; he loved to sing along with her.

Keith had a fascination with the music of Jim Morrison and the Doors. I believe he related his own addiction struggles to Jim Morrison's through the complexity of Morrison's dark, penetrating lyrics.

He was especially taken with the new Patti Austin/James Ingrim album, "Every Home Should Have One." He said his favorite song on the album, "Baby Come to Me," which he played over and over, made him think of me. Whenever I hear that song on the radio today it transports me back to that time and place in my life.

Wanting to know everything he could about me Keith often asked me questions, sometimes making a game of it. I remember both of us sitting cross-legged, facing each other on his ugly brown velour sofa (which actually was very comfortable). He said, "I'm going to ask you a question. Say the first thing that pops into your head. Don't think about it, okay? Ready?"

"Okay...go," I said.

"What is your absolute favorite song ever written?"

"All The Way, sung by Frank Sinatra." I couldn't believe that answer came out of my mouth; I don't think I had ever thought about it or said it out loud. But that emotive song had haunted me ever since I'd seen the movie "The Joker's Wild" as a child. My mother played it on the piano from time to time.

His eyes opened wide with surprise. "I can't believe you just said that! I *love* that song." We both started singing the song...*When somebody loves you it's no good unless he loves you, All The Way.* For me that brief discourse remains suspended in time. We had no idea how defining that song would be in terms of our relationship.

Soon after we began dating Keith asked me what my favorite fruit was. I told him I loved cherries but only if they were firm and dark. He surprised me the next day at my job holding a brown paper bag with two pounds of large, perfect cherries. Every single cherry was firm and dark...and washed! He'd had one of the girls at work hand pick them making absolutely sure each one was flawless. I couldn't imagine how long it took for her to sort through all the boxes in the cooler. It was the most thoughtful gift I'd ever received.

Keith and I went to see the romantic comedy "Arthur" starring Dudley Moore and Liza Minnelli the first night it was released that August. He told me later on that evening that he'd fallen deeply in love with me while watching that movie. We'd both enjoyed the film but it had especially struck an emotional chord in him.

He had such a sweet way about him, I felt like a princess in a fairy tale. He indulged me, took care of my every need. It was impossible not to adore him. I could relax, be myself, and know that he'd love me unconditionally.

The past was behind me. I had finally found the serenity and happiness I'd always dreamed about.

Fifteen: The Polaroid Picture

> *Coincidence is God's way*
> *of staying anonymous.*
> *~ Author Unknown*

K eith's father's produce market wasn't your
ordinary, run of the mill fruit and vegetable
stand. Years before he'd purchased an unremarkable little road stand and the prime property it
sat on. Before that he'd earned a modest income
from the bar he'd owned downtown.

Shortly after he'd bought the new business the
United Food and Commercial Workers Union Local
27 called a strike, forcing all the area unionized grocery stores to shut down until an agreement could
be reached. His privately owned, non-unionized
market was the only place for local residents to
shop. Within his first few months of ownership he
recouped his entire investment. The little produce
market became a booming, multi-million dollar
business. He dreamed of one day turning the business over to his sons.

As a produce buyer along with his father, Keith
worked very odd hours. The Maryland Wholesale
Produce Market in Jessup Maryland opened at ten
o'clock p.m. Sunday through Friday. The freshest
produce and best deals were had in the early hours
of the morning. Keith went to bed at seven p.m.
sharp Sunday through Thursday, setting his alarm
to wake him at two o'clock on the following morn-

ing. Each day he and his father would do all the buying for the day, go to the business, and then come home at around eleven o'clock in the morning. I still worked full-time as a credit manager from nine to five or twelve to nine five days per week. After a month of living together we got tired of our conflicting work schedules. With Keith's permission I quit my job.

With all my newly found free time I made it my project to get the badly neglected house in order. The two tiny closets on the first floor were already bursting at the seams. I decided to clear out the trash-heaped, walk-in closet upstairs and then claim it for my own. It hadn't been used in a few years, probably since Lauren had moved out. I marched in there armed with several big black trash bags and a vacuum cleaner. Then I plopped myself down on the floor and went to work.

Random papers littered the closet floor, so I began the task of separating the keepers from the trash. While going through one particular pile I came upon the back of a buried Polaroid picture. I pulled it out of the pile and flipped it over. I couldn't believe my eyes; it was a picture of me! It all came back to me when I saw the background of the picture and what I was wearing. I remembered that Lauren had taken that snapshot six years before when we'd seen each other at my high-school boyfriend's senior prom. They had been in the same graduating class. Assuming she must have left more pictures than just that one behind I searched through all the papers on the floor. I rummaged through everything but never found another snapshot.

That picture of me had been hidden in Keith's house for years and he'd never seen it; he never even knew it existed. He'd never seen my face before the night he'd first noticed me at Christopher's. What was the likelihood of that happening? It wasn't a coincidence; weird things kept happening. Clearly destiny was bringing us together.

After clearing out the closet I set my sights on the rest of the house. Keith barely knew how to change a light bulb nor was he motivated in any way to do so. Any changes would be up to me.

A lady who had worked for his family for many years came once a week to clean the house and do the laundry. I appreciated having someone do the housework--anybody but that particular lady because she reeked of body odor. Now I'm not talking about run of the mill B.O.; the noxious odor she emitted permeated the rug fibers and upholstery and clung to the walls. I'd walk in the door hours after she had left the house and the lingering stench would smack me right in the face. Holding my breath I'd bolt for the can of Lysol and saturate the air with enough fragrance to overcome her malodorous emanation. It didn't seem to bother Keith at all. He was happy as long as he had a clean house and laundered clothes.

I weighed the options of tolerating the odor or doing the housework, a chore that I despised, by myself. In the end my hypersensitive olfactory glands triumphed. She had to go. That meant one thing...I was about to become a Domestic Engineer.

I had been a pesco-vegetarian since I was nineteen years old, meaning I ate mostly vegetarian but included fish and seafood in my diet. Keith enjoyed vegetables (we had an endless supply) and fish but he definitely had a hankering for his meaty meals too. Even though it totally grossed me out to do so I'd occasionally cook meat or chicken for him to accommodate his craving. To prepare the meal, I'd first put on pink, rubber dishwashing gloves then I'd breathe through my mouth so I wouldn't barf from the smell. Meatloaf was the worst of all because I had to add eggs to the ground meat. The eggs grossed me out even more than the meat. I'd have to look away while I squished all the disgusting ingredients together with my meat-proofed hands. I only did it to please him. He treated me so well…it was the least I could do.

Sixteen: One Too Many

*All charming people, I
fancy, are spoiled. It is the
secret of their attraction.*
~ *Oscar Wilde*

I had never experienced dining out quite the way
I did with Keith. He loved to eat and money was
no object.

The first restaurant he ever took me to was The
Palmer House, a nostalgic, family owned Italian restaurant in downtown Baltimore. The restaurant was
named for the daily palm/tarot card readings made
available to its patrons. A spiritualist that sat at a table in the front gave readings upon request for fifteen dollars.

In its heyday The Palmer House had attracted
special occasion diners for elegant candlelit meals.
Faded autographed photos of by gone celebrity patrons lined the walls. The restaurant's swanky appeal had long since gone by the wayside leaving a
humbler clientele. Neighborhood regulars frequented the eatery where "everybody knew your
name." The owners had been produce customers of
Keith's father for many years. His parents ate there
practically every week. With the friendship came a
dining experience that far surpassed that of the average patron.

On the evening of my first visit to The Palmer
House we were greeted at the door with a warm

welcome then seated at a table in the back. I never saw a menu. Keith ordered all of his favorites for me to try; he liked to order a variety of dishes then take doggy bags filled with leftovers home for another day. The Palmer House's food was delicious and the portions were plentiful; the deluge of food was way more than we could eat. After dinner I had a tarot card reading. I didn't find out anything remarkable but nevertheless enjoyed the offbeat experience.

Keith was a clotheshorse. I'd never before met a guy who liked shoes more or had a larger inventory than I did. He wore *shmatehs* (rags) to work but when we went out he always looked dapper in a sport jacket and matching shoes. He once showed me a box filled with his outrageous collection of platform shoes that he'd saved from the seventies. They were the types of ostentatious shoes Elton John or Mick Jagger would have worn as part of their stage costume, only Keith had actually wore them as daily foot attire. The colors ranged from pink plaid to yellow patent leather and all the platforms were three inches or higher. I could only imagine what he must have looked like stepping out in those monstrosities. The thought of it cracked me up. He was such a trip!

Life with Keith was stimulating and fun; he added color and comic relief to my previously troubled life. He had lots of friends; his house had always been their hangout. I liked the majority of them, which was a good thing because someone was always visiting us. He had two very close friends who were brothers to each other and like brothers to him. I'd already known those guys pretty well be-

fore I'd met Keith; they had lived in my neighborhood and we'd all gone to school together. I felt
comfortable having them around the house. The
older of the two brothers lived with us for a few
months while transitioning from graduate school to
the working world.

When we were alone, Keith and I enjoyed playing backgammon together. He also liked playing
word-memory games. One game in particular began
by naming one type of animal then taking turns
adding on to the chain of words. For instance one
hen, two cows, three tigers, four giraffes, five ducks,
and so on. He had an awesome memory and could
go on and on. I on the other hand could never get
past the fifth animal. He assured me I'd get better
with practice but I never did.

His favorite alone time hobby was calculating
baseball statistics. He'd sit on the sofa with a yellow,
lined legal pad diligently making columns and lists
of complicated statistical problems to figure out.
Watching his keen mind in action I often imagined
how different his life might have been had he stayed
in school and applied himself.

I simply couldn't understand why someone
with so much potential had been hell-bent on self-
destruction. It was impossible for me to visualize
him at his worst since I'd only seen him at his best. I
never wanted to experience the silent demon that he
battled every day; I prayed that his addiction would
never resurface. I believed that I had the power to
keep him sober; if I loved him enough he'd never
want to use again.

Only one thing disturbed me. All the addiction and recovery literature that I had read stated that alcohol was a drug that compromised sobriety. Keith, a far cry from an alcoholic, had occasional drinks at restaurants, maybe more when we went out with his parents. With my low tolerance to alcohol I drank very little if at all. He assured me that I had nothing to worry about. He said that alcohol wasn't a problem for him. He said that he could handle it and from what I'd evidenced that seemed true. Still I was concerned, but since he functioned well in every aspect of his life I didn't want to place too much emphasis on the drinking issue. I hadn't had any experience when it came to addiction and didn't want to be the judge of his behavior. If he said things were okay I had to believe him.

Keith and I often dined out with his parents. I got along well with them and enjoyed their company. They were a comical, entertaining couple. I never knew what to expect from our evenings together but I always looked forward to the show.

Habitually between five and six o'clock every evening his parents would have one round of Scotch on the rocks at home. Then they'd go out to a restaurant, sit at the bar, and continue drinking Scotch until they were ready to eat dinner. The more they drank the funnier they got.

After we'd sit down at a table his parents would inevitably find a trivial point of contention to argue. Both of them loud and flagrant, they'd banter back and forth across the dinner table, neither one admitting they were wrong. Eventually realizing that no one could win, his mother would begin her storytelling. She'd recall situations from her ordinary daily affairs and exaggerate them. She thrived on attention; the more reaction she received the more outrageous the stories became. She'd repeat the same story over and over, more histrionic with each reprise. The two of them kept me in stitches!

Keith's parents lived in a beautiful high-rise condo in Baltimore and had a second home in Boca Raton, Florida. His mother enjoyed Florida much more than she did Baltimore; she spent six months of the year there. His father stayed behind with his produce business. He thrived on working hard; he didn't like being away from his business for extended periods of time.

Keith had obviously gotten his fashion sense from his father. His dad always dressed beautifully. He wore a brand new shirt every time he went out; he'd only wear a shirt once and then give it away. He had an extensive hat and shoe collection that he matched to every outfit he wore. A loud, outspoken man, he seemed intimidating but was actually as gentle as a pussycat.

His father was a generous, charitable man. He owned several cars, mostly Lincolns and Cadillacs, which he distributed among friends and family. He demanded impeccable service wherever he went but those that cared for him were heavily rewarded.

Keith's parents belonged to the very exclusive Boca Raton Hotel and Beach Club in Florida. They owned a magnificent Rolls Royce Corniche convertible that his mother drove all around Boca. His mother spent her days at the club relaxing in her private cabana or floating on her raft in the ocean or pool. She was a stunning, petite, blonde with a perpetual dark suntan. She sparkled from head to toe with diamond jewelry which included the beautiful necklace that spelled out her name in diamonds. Every stylish outfit she wore was studded with rhinestones. I'm not sure who had more hats and shoes, her or her husband. She shuffled around in back-less high heel shoes, taking small steps to keep her balance. Her perfectly manicured fingernails were never less than an inch long. Everywhere she went people knew her by name.

She had an outrageous personality. She never filtered her words, just blurted out whatever was on her mind. No subject was taboo! A very kind hearted, charitable woman, she volunteered her time and contributed a significant amount of money to animal causes.

Keith referred to his parents by their first names, never Mom and Dad. They didn't seem to mind though I thought it sounded cold and disrespectful. I think his parents had become anesthetized after going through so many painful ordeals with him; drug addiction by nature destroys the trust and respect of all relationships. But the more time we all spent together the more loving their interactions became. I saw their relationships turn around in just a few short months. With me in the picture his parents gradually let down their guard and regained a guarded level of trust with him. It touched my heart deeply the first time I heard Keith call his parents Mom and Dad. I felt it showed tremendous growth on his part.

With his parents in Baltimore, Keith swept me away for a trip to sunny Florida. I'd vacationed in Miami as a young child and spent a few days in Ft. Lauderdale, but I had never experienced the "Boca" life. I had the opportunity to walk in his mother's shoes (not literally because her feet were three sizes smaller than mine were) for one utopian week, madly in love and surrounded by swaying palm trees. We had first class accommodations at his parents' golf villa apartment on the grounds of the grandiose old Boca Raton Hotel.

As an extension of the main hotel, their apartment included maid service and clean linens daily. His mother's Rolls Royce was with her in Baltimore at the time so we drove the Lincoln Continental that remained in Florida. We went to the Beach Club every day that week. Only members or hotel guests were permitted to enter the property through the security gate. Each day we drove our car up to the gate just like VIP's, mentioned his mother's name to the security guard, and sailed right through. Then we'd do the same thing with the valet at the club and he'd park our car right up front.

Keith's parents had generously given us carte blanche with their hotel account. We'd just show the card and everything went on their bill. A waitress walked around The Beach Club taking food and beverage orders and then served them to the guests as they relaxed in their lounge chairs. The first day we were there Keith turned me on to the most lusciously irresistible piña colada I had ever tasted. We subsequently overindulged in the twelve-dollar frozen cocktails every day for the rest of the week. For lunch the dining room offered a massive, pricey salad bar as well as a variety of overpriced tropical menu items. Outside on the dining room patio a Latin guitarist serenaded the guests with calypso music.

Every evening we'd dress up and he'd take me to one of his favorite restaurants for dinner. I had the time of my life on that vacation. I tasted a lifestyle I thought I'd never be privy to and I loved every millisecond of it. Who wouldn't?

Everything was going well. I liked Keith's parents and they liked me. But there was one member of the family that I'd yet to meet.

Keith rarely mentioned his brother Mike to me. I'd never met him because he'd been locked away in prison the entire time that I'd known Keith. Nobody ever had a kind word to say about the guy so I felt no great loss.

One autumn weekday afternoon Keith and I casually took a drive to Western Maryland to see the spectacularly colored trees on the mountainside. While we were up there I suggested we stop in Hagerstown so I could show him a beautiful park I had once visited. *Greenbrier State Park*, nestled in the Appalachian Mountains had a fifty-acre lake. In the summer it offered swimming and sunbathing on its sandy beach. It was fall, the weather had turned cool, and the swimming season had ended. The air was crisp and cool but the sun felt warm, reflecting off the lake. Off-season and midweek, the expansive beach was deserted. We shared the quiet setting with one other person, a photographer trying to capture the breathtaking scenery on film.

Feeling romantic, we took off our shoes and walked hand-in-hand along the beach. The guy with the camera asked if he could take our picture. We didn't know why he wanted it but said yes, considering his request a compliment.

A few days later Keith received an unexpected collect call from the Maryland Correctional Institution. Mike called to say that when he received his weekly copy of the Hagerstown Herald-Mail our picture was on the front cover. He congratulated Keith on his new girlfriend. I thought that was kind of creepy. His brother saw me long before I met him and I didn't care if that day ever came. I pictured him as some evil dark entity; the thought made me shudder. I never asked Keith when his brother would be released. I did not look forward to that dreadful homecoming.

Seventeen: The Slip

No man is happy without a delusion of some kind. Delusions are as necessary to our happiness as realities.
~ Christian Nevell Bovee

Our family of four had settled into a happy, comfortable lifestyle together. Shane and Leon were happy having free run of the house and back yard. Keith and I both loved animals so we decided to get another dog. He thought Basset Hounds were cute because of their sad droopy eyes but I wanted something cuddlier. He agreed to go check out a litter of puppies I'd seen advertised in the paper. Once we saw the puppies we had to have one. The adorable little fur-balls were a mix of Black Labrador Retriever and Irish Setters. We already had two boys so we picked out a cute, friendly female pup and brought her home.

Her sweet little face inspired the name Honeybell. We named her after our favorite orange. Shane seemed a bit unnerved when he first saw her but she soon became his best friend. Lazy Leon couldn't have cared less as long as she didn't try to sniff his butt. He hid most of the time anyway. Before we knew it our little black puffball had turned into a man-size dog. On her two feet she stood as tall as we did. She loved to jump up and put her big paws on our shoulders. She would hang on while we danced with her. Where Shane was hyper, Honeybell did everything in slow motion. She could stretch out one simple lick on the face for five long slobbery seconds.

Shane and Honeybell both liked to swim with us in the pool. They'd shed so much fur that we'd have to skim all the loose hairs off the water surface so the filter wouldn't clog. At night they'd find a comfortable space in the king-sized bed with us, sprawled out on their backs with their feet in the air. Our little "family" had grown and we'd established ourselves as a couple. We were both wholeheartedly invested in our future together.

Keith asked me to get a part-time job. It had nothing to do with money; he just wanted me to use my time more productively. I had no case to argue. He suggested working as a cashier at his father's produce market. I agreed to give it a shot.

Long story short, I hated that job. In an effort not to show favoritism among his employees Keith patronized me. I didn't appreciate his condescending tone, nor did I enjoy freezing my *tuchis* off while standing on the cold, concrete slab for hours at a time. The cashiering was fun but in my idle time I had to trim up vegetables and package spinach, among other things. The cold, wet, dirty spinach came in boxes. I had to reach my hands into that muck and make up one pound bags for sale. My fingers froze and my fingertips shriveled up. Wet, sandy grime imbedded under my fingernails. I detested *everything* about that filthy task.

I've since coined the phrase, "Jewish girls don't sweep!" I never even had that notion until I was handed a broom at the produce market and told to sweep the floor. Everyone laughed at my bumble-headed attempt. Truth-be-told I had never swept anything sizable before.

I knew how to vacuum but I had very little experience sweeping with a broom. Although I've become a more proficient sweeper over the years I still get blisters on my dainty hands every single time!

I was used to working in offices where my hands stayed clean and my toes didn't turn into ice cubes. My prior work experience was in bookkeeping so that's where I directed my search.

I found a part-time job working in the home office of a Baltimore based retail sports apparel chain. Two friendly young women worked in the office full time; I already knew one of the women from high school. The environment was upbeat and I didn't have to travel far to get there.

Since Keith was home all day his friends often came over to hang out with him. I'd come home around two o'clock on my working days and then we'd spend the rest of the afternoon together.

When I came home from work one afternoon I walked in the front door and found the house in shambles. My first thought was that our house had been robbed and ransacked. It appeared as if a cyclone had raged through the living room.

Our potted palm tree was lying on its side with its dirt spilled out onto the carpet. A hanging picture had crashed onto the floor, glass broken and fragments perilously scattered. The empty frame from the glass-topped coffee table was on its side, leaning against the mirrored wall. Its quarter inch thick, broken glass-top leaned next to it. While I was engrossed in surveying the damage, Keith stumbled in from the bedroom, his glassy eyes trying to focus and his drooping eyelids struggling to stay open.

"I'm sorrr...ry, I messs...sed uuup...we broke the cof...fee taaa...ble," he slowly droned on, obviously doped up and struggling to get the words out. In that instant my dream turned into a nightmare. I felt totally betrayed.

"Look at you, you're completely fucked up," I cried out in disbelief!

"So what ... I... had... a slip. It haaa...pens to ev...ry...body," he defended with muddleheaded conviction.

"Look what you did," I shouted through heavy sobs! "You're sickening!"

My impassioned words landed on deaf ears; he was too incoherent to reason with. I somberly watched as he staggered over to the sofa, plopped down, then slumped over and passed out. I ran to the bedroom, sprawled out on the bed, and dissolved into tears. I cried until my stomach was sick and my eyes were swollen shut. Suffering alone the pain seemed unbearable. The one person I had always counted on was now the source of my agony, and he lay bombed out and drooling on the living room sofa.

I didn't know his specific cohorts but I could have easily guessed. He still had a few Quaalude using friends and there was no mistaking the obnoxious "luded-out" behavior. I was incensed! I couldn't understand why a "friend" would sell drugs to a recovering addict. Didn't they care about his sobriety?

As devastating as that scenario was I couldn't bring myself to give up on him for one exercise in poor judgment. I only hoped that the sober realization of the pain he had caused me would quash any future compulsions to use. And from that point on I'd shower him with enough love to insure his desire to stay straight for me. He had given so much of himself to me; now it was time for me to stick by him and prove my love.

When he came out of his drug haze I poured out my heart to him. I had to make him understand how the sight of him in that doped-up state had crushed me. I wanted him to console me, promise I'd never have to suffer through that hell again. He held me and deeply apologized for hurting me in that way. It was such a relief to have him back to normal, to share my feelings with him. My sweetheart would surely promise he'd never do that to me again. He'd tell me that he loved me too much to ever hurt me and that our relationship meant more to him than any drug possibly could. But even as he painfully witnessed my suffering, he could not in good conscience promise me any of those things. He was first and foremost a drug addict and therefore lived his life one day at a time.

Eighteen: Only Shooting Water

Through pride we are deceiving ourselves. But deep down below the surface of the average conscience a small, still voice says to us, something is out of tune.
~ Carl Jung

After the Quaalude incident we resumed our life as if nothing had happened. As far as I could tell Keith had gotten back on track with his sobriety and I tried to forget that whole ugly mess. I just wanted to move forward in our relationship. We had so much going for us and an exciting future ahead. We shared so many dreams. Things just had to work out…they just had to.

But I found it hard to view him the same way as I did before. I had seen Keith's other personality and I didn't like it. I loved everything about "Normal Keith," but his flip side scared me. A stranger had stood before me that dreadful afternoon and I hated him. He was not welcome back.

I didn't understand the power of addiction. I believed that drug abuse was a choice. And if given the choice between self-destruction and our loving relationship he'd surely choose the latter. That was pure logic…I just couldn't see the situation any other way.

We both wanted his relapse kept off the record. I didn't want to share that experience with anyone for two reasons, to protect his image and to protect mine. Most people wouldn't have understood why I would remain in a relationship like that. But I had given my heart to him and my commitment to our relationship. He was my future... I couldn't imagine that our relationship would ever be beyond repair.

Our roles were reversing. He needed my support and I believed that his needs were far more important than mine were. He knew he had a devoted friend and a steadfast ally in me. He often asserted that if we were to have an adult relationship the details of our life must remain private. That sounded so romantic... like it was the two of us against the world.

From time to time Keith would go out early in the evening to play racquetball. When he'd come home he'd always hang his canvas gym bag on the doorknob leading down to the basement. One morning I had gathered up a load of towels to wash and was heading downstairs to the laundry room. When I opened the door and spotted his gym bag I figured I'd check to see if anything inside of it needed washing. I unzipped the bag and looked inside. The bag was mostly empty except for a hypodermic needle that was lying on the bottom. I was shocked and horrified; I knew that there could only be one explanation. Keith was shooting up again.

Keith wasn't home to confront. I glared at my insidious rival. I agonized over the implication of the evidence. As my anger and despair escalated, I found myself pacing the floors in a stupor. My moment of truth hung in limbo as I slowly drowned in a sea of angst.

When Keith finally walked in the door I ambushed him with the evidence in hand. Unhinged after obsessing for hours I cried out, "You've been shooting up again. How could you do that to me?"

He didn't appear flustered by the confrontation just concerned with my mania. "Shhhh...calm down. It's not what you think. Everything is okay. Give me a chance to explain," he said in a soothing voice.

"Explain? What is there to explain? There's only one reason why you'd have a needle," I screamed, frenzied.

"Shhh...listen. It's okay. I'm not using," he began to explain. Feeling some relief after hearing his encouraging statement I stopped screaming and gave him a chance to plead his case. "I know you'll find this hard to believe but I only used water. When I got off heroin I never lost the urge to feel the needle. That's all I did, I promise. You have nothing to worry about. It will all be okay. Please don't be upset."

I felt guilty for misjudging him. He was obviously struggling with his sobriety and needed my understanding.

His explanation eased my mind even though the thought of what he had just revealed to me was very disturbing. I took him at his word without questioning the validity of his reasoning. Poking holes in his story could mean the demise of our relationship. I didn't want that to happen. As long as "Normal

Keith" stood before me, I chose to look the other way.

Oddly after the day of that disclosure he began testing my devotion by posing "What if" questions. He suddenly seemed to be feeling insecure about our relationship. I hated the drills; some of the questions unnerved me, though I never let on. I answered him the way I thought he'd want me to so he'd feel secure. The most disturbing question he asked me was, "If I ever got locked up, would you be there for me…no matter what?" I couldn't imagine that ever happening and assured him I'd be there for him…no matter what.

One morning while Keith was at work, I climbed the stepstool looking for something I'd shoved in the back of the highest kitchen cabinet. Standing on the third step I was able to peer straight into the bottom shelf of the cabinet. Lying on the edge just inside the door was another hypodermic needle. I could tell that he'd reached up there in a hurry barely getting his fingers past the edge. And unlike the gym bag incident he had made a considerable effort to hide the evidence.

The shock of seeing another syringe sent me spiraling into panic. I knew I'd have to wait to confront him again.

When he finally walked through the front door after I'd fervently obsessed for hours, my pent up anxiety exploded like a time bomb. Brandishing the incriminating evidence I blindsided him.

He remained perfectly composed like he had the time before and even used the same lame "water" excuse. I questioned his alibi but no matter how hard I pushed he wouldn't admit to anything.

Though I was overcome with my own pain and disappointment I brushed my feelings aside. I'd be okay; it was him I had to worry about. I told myself that I'd just have to try harder to keep him happy and be more diligent in keeping him away from the drugs. I felt that I was stronger and far better equipped to shoulder that burden than he was.

Not able to recall any recent telltale signs of drug abuse, I asked him if he was still clean once more for reassurance then looked the other way...again.

Nineteen: Girls Night on the Block

> *There is nothing wrong with making mistakes. Just don't respond with an encore.*
> *~ Author Unknown*

I felt a rapid dissolution of the stable, secure foundation I had come to rely on in my relationship with Keith. My life was no longer about me; it was centered on trying to fix his problems. Knowing that my entire world could crash down around me at any time, I lived every moment stressed out and worried.

Keith had become noticeably irresponsible; his actions often landed him in trouble. I kept finding speeding tickets haphazardly lying around the house. He had also amassed a collection of parking tickets. He didn't see any of that as a problem; his lawyer always managed to have those things "taken care of."

Keith's attorney was also a well-respected Baltimore County Councilman. His public service position afforded him lots of privileges and favors. Keith explained to me that his attorney used those perks to defend his premium clients, sacrificing his low-income clients in exchange. His reputation was well known among young, white-collar drug offenders who relied on him to have their charges dismissed.

I found Keith's willful disregard for the law frustrating. I couldn't understand why he didn't flinch in the face of the law. The mere thought of being in trouble scared me to death. Though I often pleaded for him clean up his life, he smugly continued to buck the system. He refused to listen to my logic; I just didn't get it. He'd confidently assert that he had everything under control. It never looked that way to me but I'd never had to deal with the court system. I had no experience in that area. He was streetwise; maybe he knew something that I didn't know. All I could do was watch and worry.

My girlfriend Julie owned a house in our neighborhood and we'd get together from time to time. I'd known her since elementary school. On an evening when I knew that Keith had other plans, Julie and I arranged for a "girls' night out." We decided to spend the evening downtown at the Baltimore Inner Harbor having dinner and walking around. She offered to drive.

Keith was still at home when Julie arrived to pick me up. He wasn't sure what time he was going to leave. I said goodbye and told him to have a good time. We went back to Julie's house for a little while then headed downtown.

The intersecting streets joining the two pavilions of the Baltimore Inner Harbor are Pratt Street and Light Street. They are wide, high-traffic boulevards. Across from the pavilions on the other side of Light Street stands the luxurious Baltimore Hyatt Hotel.

The Hyatt Hotel's garage location was a convenient place for us to park that night. As we made the right turn from Pratt onto Light, I noticed a green

Pontiac Lemans that looked just like mine sitting on the opposite side of the road. Police cruisers were parked in front of it and behind it with lights flashing. Appearing abandoned, the car rested alongside the curb in the right turn lane. Signs indicated that parking was prohibited there. I asked Julie to U-turn and drive me across the street. Keith hadn't asked or had any reason to use my car that night but I had a very bad feeling that he was in trouble.

She pulled her car behind the police cruiser and I jumped out. I looked at the license plate on the Lemans and confirmed my suspicion. It was my car. I approached the officer and asked him to explain what was going on. His explanation was detailed but all I heard was D.U.I. and that my car was going to be impounded. He said that the gentleman driving the car had been arrested; another squad car had recently transported him to Central Booking. I was furious. He'd been laying the groundwork with his commitment drillings. I felt manipulated and used.

I didn't know the first thing about bailing someone out of jail nor did I have the cash to do so. I considered leaving him there to sweat it out for awhile but I was fearful of his retaliatory anger. Anyway, how could I renege on the promise I'd made to him when he needed me the most?

When Julie offered to write a check and loan me the money I figured that I'd better come to his rescue.

Central Booking was not a place that two young woman in their twenties should ever find themselves late at night. The courthouse was located in the heart of the most depraved part of town infamously known as "The Block," and well known for its variety of strip clubs, porno shops, and peep shows. Perverts, prostitutes, and vagabonds walked the streets at all hours of the night.

We found a parking space up the street, and then scurried toward the courthouse passing a string of homeless people who were sleeping on the sidewalk. Other indigents sat on the steps in front of the courthouse building panhandling for money. I never imagined I'd ever end up in a place or situation like that.

After we'd waited for hours the magistrate finally processed Keith and set his bail. Julie paid for his release and we all headed home. I have no recollection of what I actually said to him that night but I do remember his attitude. He never thanked me; in fact he didn't seem the least bit grateful for my help. Apparently bailing him out was part of our agreement and therefore expected of me.

In the days that followed I tried everything I could think of to make him understand the proportions of my despair. I pleaded, cried, rationalized and threatened. I even tried to intellectualize addiction from his viewpoint, examining the depths of his mind to understand the cause of his relapse. If I knew what the cues were maybe I could change the script. But all I learned was that he had no insight to share. There was no rationalization. Addiction was a primal, all-consuming urge that he struggled with every minute of every day.

We had shared so many beautiful dreams together and I wasn't ready for those dreams to die. I believed that we were meant to be together and I was determined to do whatever it took to make our relationship work. The wonderful guy that still remained inside of the addict was drowning and I had to save him. If only he would trust me enough to reveal the delusional thoughts that poisoned his mind I could help him to stay straight. As I often did in childhood, I desperately tried to apply logic to an obviously illogical situation.

Keith threw me a bone and promised to trust me more with his feelings. That was good enough for me.

Twenty: California Nightmare

It is foolish to tear one's hair in grief, as though sorrow would be made less by baldness.
~ Cicero

Whether intended or not, Keith kept me off balance and confused. Things were never as they seemed. I didn't know whether to trust my observations or believe his excuses. Each point of view demonstrated degrees of validity. One thing for sure, I no longer trusted him.

I kept our problems hidden in a private vault, often making excuses for his behavior. In a desperate attempt to hold on to my relationship with Keith I averted conflict with him whenever possible. I believed if I did and said everything right, our relationship would get back on track. That meant keeping him under my watchful eye every possible minute of every day. The oppressive burden fostered my withdrawal from friends and family.

Though unaware, I'd become entangled in the web of co-dependency.

Keith seemed able to sustain weeks of sobriety before relapsing. Dreading the next slip I lived teetering on the emotional edge.

We'd gone downtown to Little Italy one evening to dine at one of our favorite restaurants. We ordered our usual meals; two house salads and two baked rigatonis, well done. Halfway into the meal I got up to use the ladies room, leaving him sitting alone. When I returned to the table Keith was face down in his plate of baked rigatoni. I called his name and he looked up at me, covered with tomato sauce, in a drugged out stupor. It sounds hilarious but I was *not* laughing.

Humiliated and furious I told him that I was leaving and would take a cab home. Even in his drugged out haze he managed to pull rank on me; he threatened that if I left him there I'd better find another place to live. I was afraid to call his bluff. I motioned for the waiter to bring the check so we could leave as quickly as possible. I paid the bill and stormed away from the table. He stood up and followed me, stumbling and weaving the entire way.

The valet brought our car to the front of the restaurant and Keith fell into the front passenger seat. Then, along side of my bombed-out boyfriend but all alone with my heartache, I drove silently home.

He apologized the next day, professed his undying love for me and promised to try harder. That's all it took to keep me coming back for more.

Each week Keith would give me money to pay the bills and then I'd write checks from my personal Union Trust checking account. When they started offering a bounce-free checking service, I signed up for the option. In the event my account became overdrawn, a ten-thousand-dollar loan with interest would be generated to cover the checks. With excellent record keeping and perfect credit I had no intention of letting that happen. I took it as a precautionary measure only.

When I opened up my bank statement one month I saw that the ten-thousand-dollar loan had kicked in. Assuming it was their error I flipped through the returned checks they'd mailed back with my statement. One check had been signed with my name but written in Keith's handwriting for ten-thousand-dollars. The check number was out of sequence; it had come from the middle of a surplus pad that I'd kept in my desk drawer. I hit the ceiling.

I called Keith at work to interrogate him. He readily admitted to writing the check but said that we needed the money and that he would pay the loan right back. Then putting his trademark spin on the issue he argued that I shouldn't even have that feature if I never planned to use it. He tried his best to make my anger seem unwarranted. But I didn't care what he said or what intimidation tactics he used; he'd been caught red-handed. Nothing he could say would justify the deceit.

My blood was boiling. An overpowering urge to run away took over... and I wanted revenge. If I left without a trace before he got home he'd have to worry about me for a change. I'd go as far away as I possibly could so he couldn't find me. I immediately got on the phone and arranged for a flight to San Diego that left in a few hours. I could stay with my sister once I got there. My bags were packed and in no time I was gone.

No one including my sister knew of my plans; I didn't want anyone to stop me. By early evening I'd be on the other side of the country. I definitely didn't want Keith to know my whereabouts and he'd have my parents singing like canaries if they had any information. They were like putty in his hands. My parents would just have to worry for a little while. When I arrived in San Diego I would surprise Marlene, and then call them to explain what happened and swear them to silence.

My main objective in leaving the way I did was to shake Keith up. After being repressed by his domination I'd enjoy having the upper hand, leaving him hanging in suspension for the duration of my choosing. Maybe then he'd understand the magnitude of my suffering.

Meanwhile as I relaxed on my cross-country flight, all hell was breaking loose at home. Keith had lost his house key that day and came home expecting me to let him in. It pissed him off when I wasn't there and he had to climb in through the window. Just as I had suspected he called my parents right away looking for me. They didn't know where I was and began to worry.

As soon as I possibly could I called my parents to let them know that I was safe. They told me that Keith was very worried and that I should call him. I stipulated that I'd keep in close contact with them if they promised to zip their lips. Although reluctant, they agreed.

With each passing day the messages Keith conveyed through my parents became more pitiful. I knew he was trying to weaken their resolve and gain their sympathy. After three days of them begging me to call him I decided to let them off the hook.

His tune totally changed when he spoke to me directly. He pummeled me with three days of pent-up anger. Threatening to kick me out of the house was his only ammunition but I did not budge. After trying that strategy for one more day he threw in the towel and began negotiating for my return. I had him exactly where I wanted him; now I was in control.

It sounds crazy but I missed him and wanted to go home. My heart ached for the person I had fallen in love with. I just wanted him to get well, for things to return to normal. For the umpteenth time he professed his undying love for me, said he couldn't survive without me. He said all the words I needed to hear, trying to convince me to give him another chance. It worked; I packed my suitcase and headed home.

My plane landed at Friendship Airport (now BWI/Thurgood Marshall) early in the evening. I rushed to the payphone, excited to tell Keith that I was back. He answered the phone with a groggy-sounding voice, saying he'd been sleeping. I told him I'd get my luggage and my car and then come right home.

While in sunny California I hadn't given a thought to Baltimore's weather. But it was the dead of winter and the city was buried under a fresh blanket of heavily falling snow. I hopped off the parking shuttle carrying my suitcases and trudged through the snow to my car with my sandals on. I didn't have gloves so I had to wipe the snow off my car with my bare hands. My hands ached and my bare toes were numb from exposure to the freezing-cold snow.

I couldn't wait to warm up my car and go home. But when I got to the highway it looked like an ice skating rink. Trucks and cars were sliding and skidding all over the place and the rapidly falling snow reduced visibility to about one hundred feet. Petrified but determined to make it home I shifted my gears into low and painstakingly inched along the highway.

With snow piling up on my front windshield faster than the wipers could remove it and no visibility out the snow covered side or back windows, I soon realized that I'd never make the entire twenty mile trek home. The roads were getting worse not better. Road crews had not yet plowed or salted the highway and the snow continued to build up on it. Staying on the highway meant imminent danger. I'd have to find the closest hotel to stay at for the night; I prayed that I'd get there in one piece. The whole experience seemed like a nightmare. I couldn't help but wonder if it was my punishment for having run away.

Howard Johnson's on Route 40 West was the nearest hotel I could think of. As I exited the highway the Howard Johnson's sign ahead was like a beacon of light to a ship lost at sea. Everyone driving ahead of me had the same idea; they were all turning into the Howard Johnson's parking lot. I worried that the hotel would be booked for the night but it wasn't so I checked into a room.

Three long hours had passed since Keith had last heard from me. Surely he'd be worried sick. As soon as I got into my room I called him. After a few rings he answered the telephone with the same groggy-sounding voice as before saying again that he'd been sleeping. He didn't have a clue about the blizzard that had besieged Baltimore or that three hours had passed since he'd last heard from me. Hungering for consolation I detailed my perilous adventure. His feeble attempt to comfort me while yawning was not the response I'd hoped for. I said I'd be home tomorrow and I hung up the phone.

Alone in that dark unfamiliar room I was crestfallen and profoundly lonely. I had gone from euphoric empowerment to insufferable guilt. Silent tears streamed down my face. I felt painfully unappreciated yet blamed myself for creating the mess. It seemed his transgressions significantly paled in comparison to mine. I concluded that I'd gotten exactly what I deserved. There would be no resolution that night. I looked forward to our joyful reunion the next day.

Twenty-One: The Backgammon Game

You can never cross the ocean unless you have the courage to lose sight of the shore.
~ *Christopher Columbus*

"Relationships don't just happen. They take work." I don't know exactly where I heard that advice but the concept had stuck to my psyche like burs to a cotton sock. I'm pretty sure I misconstrued the guiding principle though because my interpretation evolved into, "Relationships are burdensome and backbreaking. Like war they are only won with blood, sweat, and tears!"

I had taken on this responsibility and would see it through till the end. It never occurred to me that my needs were just as important as Keith's needs or that I'd lose myself in the process. After all nothing was wrong with me; he was the one with the problems. I believed that I had enough endurance to undertake the fixing of Keith. I'd just have to find the right approach.

Our relationship went into a honeymoon phase after I came home from California. We even took a three-day trip to Florida. We had a good time but every single night Keith felt ill. He'd spend hours in the bathtub sweating out his fever and vomiting from nausea. He said he probably had some kind of virus. It definitely looked that way to me. Oddly he seemed fine during the day. Looking back from a more knowledgeable vantage point I'm sure he was suffering the effects of withdrawal.

After returning home from Florida, as far as I could tell, Keith continued holding it together. Either that or he was doing a good job of hiding his problem. We never discussed his sobriety. I allowed myself the luxury of basking in the glory of our drama-free life. Friends frequently stopped by and in our alone time we played backgammon. I never abandoned my sleuthing tendencies but I didn't spend as much time worrying.

One afternoon in the middle of one of our backgammon games there was a knock at the door. Keith got up from the sofa then opened the door and greeted a casual friend who was standing there. He led his friend right back to the kitchen, mentioning to me as he passed by that he'd be right back to finish our game. Only a few minutes passed before he walked his friend back to the front door and said goodbye. Then he sat back down and we resumed our game.

About fifteen minutes later I noticed a distinct change in his demeanor. His eyes started looking heavy and his speech slowed down. Within a very short time he started slurring his speech and his eyelids kept drifting closed. There was no mistaking the "Keith on Quaaludes" affectations.

"Your piece-of-shit friend came here just to sell you Quaaludes, didn't he?" I bitterly alleged.

"I can't arr...gue with you. You're de...fi...nitely right," he moronically droned.

"That's it, it's over. I've had enough. I'm leaving!" I shoved the backgammon board at him and stood up.

"Don't leave!" he pleaded.

Like a crazed animal I ran around the house, grabbing whatever belonged to me then made several trips loading up my car. All the while he tried over and over to stand up without falling so he could get to the front door and block it. He was crying and kept pleading with me not to leave him. I had nothing more to say.

By the time I finished loading up all of my belongings he had managed to get out the front door and crawl down two sets of concrete steps. I found him lying on the sidewalk next to my car. "You caaaan't leeeave me!" he cried out.

Ignoring his pleas I got in my car, locked the doors, and turned on the engine. I watched in disgust as he crawled on his hands and knees off the curb and into the middle of the street behind my car. As I pulled away I looked in my rear-view mirror and saw him on all fours hopelessly trying to crawl up the street after my car. It was the most pitiful site I'd ever seen but I couldn't be moved. I'd finally reached my saturation point. I drove away leaving him lying in the street crying his eyes out.

I drove directly to my parents' house which was only a mile away. My parents welcomed me in with open arms. I didn't know whether to cry or punch a hole in the wall. I regurgitated the saga that of course shocked and troubled them. Though I was their number one priority, they still loved Keith. He was Jewish and that had automatically earned him innumerable brownie points. But his lovable, charismatic personality is what sealed the deal with them.

Deeply distressed themselves they tried hard to understand the secret life that I'd been leading. I told them that Keith was an incorrigible drug addict. I said that his addiction was destroying me and that I refused to ever go back to him. I explained that I deeply loved him and this was not easy for me, but for my safety and my sanity I had to stay away from him.

I needed my parents to band together and become my pillar of strength. Knowing that hearing his voice would weaken my resolve I gave them strict orders not to ever put his calls through to me. I needed time to build up emotional strength before I could resist his sweet-talking, manipulative ways. Counting heavily on their support I made them promise not to let me talk to him.

With my father's help I unloaded my car and brought my things into the house. Then I went upstairs to my old bedroom, closed the door, and fell to pieces.

After sobering up Keith began relentlessly calling my parents' house. My father fielded several calls without involving me, but my parents lacked the experience and fortitude to stand up to him. Preying on their compassion, Keith confessed his transgressions and asked for their forgiveness. He succeeded in softening them up; they bought his sob story hook, line, and sinker. After only a few days they were begging me to take his calls. I had barely stopped crying let alone started the healing process.

I was sitting in the kitchen one morning with my father when the telephone rang. My father answered it; I could immediately tell by the sympathetic tone of his voice that Keith was on the other end. He looked at me with pleading eyes, and pointed to the receiver.

Keith knew exactly what he was doing. My parents were putty in his hands; they were too malleable to be my fortress of protection. I had no choice but to reclaim my command post. Knowing full well that I was doomed, I finally decided to take his call.

I motioned for my father to hand me the receiver. He said, "Hold on Keith, I'll let you talk to her."

"Hello Keith," I said, deliberately conveying by my tone that I was less than enthusiastic.

"Hi Baby," his voice was soft, and smooth as silk. "I'm so sorry for all the pain I've caused you. I haven't stopped crying since you left me. I love you more than I've ever loved anything or anyone...I can't live without you. Please come back to me. Tell me what I need to do... I'll do whatever you say. Just please come back."

I spelled out all the conditions of my return; I insisted on long-term outpatient therapy and daily NA (Narcotics Anonymous) meetings. I made it clear that if he screwed up I'd leave and never look back. He said he promised to do whatever it took to keep me in his life.

And I went back to him...again.

Twenty-Two: Good Luck

*The trouble with some women is
that they get all excited about
nothing – and then marry him.*
~ Cher

Keith immediately started seeing an addiction therapist and religiously attending NA meetings. He made tremendous progress with those support systems behind him. I occasionally met with the therapist to get updates. He felt that Keith was doing everything he needed to do and was working his program to stay clean. I was more than proud of him for keeping up his end of the bargain. He soon chalked up five months of sobriety.

I finally had him back. A huge weight had been lifted off of my shoulders. Between the professional support of his therapist and the tenets of the twelve-step program I found myself mostly removed from the equation. Through teamwork our relationship strengthened and grew in a positive direction. We looked forward to spending our lives together.

Don't get me wrong, I knew that anything could trigger a relapse, but I believed wholeheartedly that he was well worth the risk. I had to remain positive, looking only toward the future and not dwelling on the past. Reliving those nightmares only depressed and exhausted me. That wasn't good for either one of us.

We'd met in the spring of 1981 and it was now the spring of 1982. As I'm recalling the story I find it incredulous that so much had transpired in just twelve months. At the time it seemed like an eternity. But our relationship had survived and we made it to our one-year anniversary.

Keith made reservations at one of the best restaurants in Baltimore, The Prime Rib, to celebrate our milestone. He selected well; they served delicious food with impeccable service in a romantic, upscale atmosphere.

We had so much to celebrate that evening: our love, the growth of our relationship, our anniversary, and his sobriety. And before dinner ended there would be one more commemoration. Along with my cappuccino and scrumptious dessert came a marriage proposal and a gorgeous engagement ring. I said yes without hesitation. He slipped the ring on my finger and everyone around us applauded.

It was true--love did conquer all! My love, devotion, and understanding had finally fixed him. I viewed the marriage proposal as his commitment to me to stay straight. I was going to have that Fairy Tale ending after all. We'd ride off into the sunset and live happily ever after.

At the time of our engagement I was twenty-three years old and Keith was twenty-six. Twenty-three seemed to be the age of commitment for many of my friends who'd already become engaged or newly married. Like most brides-to-be I couldn't wait to begin planning my wedding.

My family enthusiastically supported our engagement. Having already chosen to overlook Keith's sordid past; my parents happily welcomed him and his parents into our family. But when I sat down alone with Keith's mother to discuss the wedding plans she asked me why I wanted to marry her son. I told her I loved him very much. I'll never forget her words. She said, "Marry him and believe me your love will turn to hate." *Ouch!*

Considering time off from work for a honeymoon, Keith helped me choose the wedding date. We chose November 28th of the same year, 1982. That gave me six months to make all the arrangements. He left all the details up to me--except one. Neither he nor his parents were willing to walk down the aisle. They thought it would be hypocritical that being his second marriage. I had no bargaining power with that provision. I'd have to think of a creative way to get them all under the *chupah* (Jewish bridal canopy) with me.

My mother and I made all the plans. We arranged for a Sunday morning wedding at Martin's West, a highly reputed, all-inclusive catering facility in Baltimore. We decided on a traditional but lavish Jewish-style Sunday morning brunch. Both the ceremony and reception would be held there but in two different rooms.

Unlike most every other girl on the planet I never envisioned myself in a traditional wedding gown. I thought they looked silly. Besides I couldn't justify the exorbitant expense of buying an overpriced dress that I'd never wear again. I pictured myself in the fashion of an 1890's Victorian lady; long white lace dress with a matching lace hat. I found the perfect outfit in a bridal store; it was a bride's-maid dress not a bridal gown and much less expensive.

I also didn't see the point of having my sisters and girlfriends spend money on dresses they would never wear again. So I asked Michele, who was married, to be my matron of honor and let her decide what she wanted to wear. She would be my only attendant.

The next thing to do was select a rabbi to perform our marriage ceremony. Keith's family had no affiliation with a synagogue and I didn't find my parents' rabbi particularly warm and fuzzy. My mother had heard about a young reform rabbi who was progressive and highly revered by his congregation. I met with him, liked him, and decided to have him officiate at our wedding. He asked me to arrange for a pre-marriage counseling session with him to get to know both of us and discuss life as a married Jewish couple.

Keith and I met with the rabbi in his study. He asked us many thought-provoking questions and looked perturbed by some of Keith's answers. I don't remember the specific questions or answers; I only recall the rabbi looking at me before we left shaking his head from side to side and sarcastically saying, "Good luck!" The next time we would see him would be on our wedding day.

I worried a bit about our first dance as husband and wife. Without question our song would be "All The Way." But we'd never danced together and I thought he'd step all over my toes. I gingerly suggested taking ballroom dancing lessons. He actually liked the idea so I signed up for the minimum number of lessons; just enough to meld our dancing styles together and safeguard my little "tootsies." Keith's female instructor taught him how to lead. Together we learned to dance the Foxtrot. By our wedding date we'd be ready to gracefully glide around the dance floor in front of all our guests.

After tossing around a few ideas we decided to honeymoon in Hawaii. A travel agent helped us plan our itinerary. We would visit three islands while we were there, Oahu, Maui, and the big island of Hawaii. Keith said money was not an issue so we reserved rooms in three of the best hotels on the islands. The grand total of the trip was $5,000. He didn't flinch.

In those days brides and grooms often changed into "going away outfits" near the end of the wedding reception. My mother took me downtown to her favorite dress shop to look for an outfit. I fell in love with a silvery-gray dress trimmed in red and black. When Keith saw my dress he decided to match his outfit to mine. I found a black patent leather open-toe pump trimmed with red piping to match my dress. Keith being Keith, he bought himself bright red leather shoes!

I figured out a way to handle the unique bridal procession. Keith would already be standing, waiting for me at the end of the aisle. His parents would wait on the side of the *bima*/stage. Then after my parents had walked down the aisle, his parents would walk up the stairs to the *chupah*. That plan didn't seem too awkward and everybody agreed on it.

Six months quickly passed while I busied myself with all the planning. Before we knew it November had arrived and Sunday the twenty-eighth was upon us. Everything went as planned. We had a beautiful ceremony and a lovely reception.

After we were introduced into the ballroom as Mr. and Mrs. we danced the Foxtrot to our song, "All The Way." We probably looked ridiculous dancing around the floor so stiff and proper but we were very proud of our accomplishment. And when all was said and done my white lace shoes stayed spotless and my feet unscathed.

I overheard a few complaints about the food coming from a table of some of our non-Jewish guests. They were all planning to eat at McDonald's after the wedding was over. Apparently they didn't know what to make of a meal consisting of cold fish and bagels. We also had an omelet station to bridge the gap between the experienced and non-experienced lox eaters. By contrast our Jewish guests *fressed* like there was no tomorrow.

As the reception was coming to a close Keith and I quietly slipped out of the room, went upstairs to the bridal suite, and changed into our matching "going away" outfits. Then we re-entered the reception hall and surprised all of our guests.

Everyone started laughing and pointing to Keith's feet. I found myself totally upstaged by his red shoes. I was laughing too. I didn't mind him having the limelight; that was Keith's signature style and one of the things I loved best about him.

We had planned to spend our wedding night at a hotel and then leave for Hawaii first thing in the morning. When the wedding reception ended I handed all the gift envelopes to my father to take home for us. He gathered up our gifts and any miscellaneous clothing like my wedding gown to safeguard until we returned from our honeymoon. We got into the limo that awaited us at the front door, posed for a few last shots, then waved goodbye and literally rode happily off into the sunset.

Twenty-Three: An Omen

*The difficulty with marriage is
that we fall in love with a personality, but must live with a character.*
~ *Peter Devries*

On the Monday morning following our wedding, we boarded the 747 jet airplane that
would fly us across the country. We had one
scheduled layover in Los Angeles. Marlene had scheduled the same flight back to Los Angeles so she shared
the first leg of our journey with us. It gave me some extra quality time to spend with her before she went back
home to San Diego.

After our brief layover in L.A., Keith and I boarded
the second plane that would take us to our honeymoon
destination, Oahu. Caught up in newlywed rapture, all
the while strapped into our unyielding airline seats, we
reminisced about our wedding day. Our guests had
been more than generous with their monetary gifts. I
was excited to have the considerable sum of money to
deposit into the new joint bank account that I planned
to open.

We had never actually outlined our financial plans
but that wasn't unusual; Keith made the money and I
paid the bills. So when he informed me on the plane to
Hawaii that all the wedding gift money would be used
to pay for our honeymoon I was blindsided. I couldn't
believe he hadn't mentioned anything during the plan-

ning of the "spare no expense" honeymoon--or at all. He wondered where I expected the money to come from as if it should have been obvious to me. I consoled myself with the possibility that I was out of line, maybe greedy. He'd done worse things before. Though extremely disappointed I had to let it go.

We were exhausted after twelve hours of traveling, but felt revived after driving our rental car around sunny Honolulu. We planned to stay on Oahu three nights and four days and didn't want to waste a second.

Many popular Waikiki Beach hotels were lined up along Kalakana Avenue. Our hotel, The Hilton Hawaiian Village Beach Resort, was sprawled out on twenty-two oceanfront acres on the northern most end of the beach. The resort was very private and afforded a majestic view of Diamond Head Mountain. The paradisiacal property included a beachfront lagoon, tropical gardens with exotic wildlife, and mesmerizing waterfalls.

We wanted to commemorate the first night of our honeymoon with a romantic dinner at a fine restaurant. The hotel Concierge recommended a five-star restaurant and made an eight o'clock reservation for that evening. We'd have a few hours to rest and recuperate.

The restaurant was intimate and the food was expertly prepared. Prawns were listed as a special entrée that evening; the description sounded delicious so I ordered it. Keith ordered Prime Rib and shared some of my jumbo prawns. By the time we had finished our dinners we were spent. We went back to our hotel looking forward to a rejuvenating sleep.

I suddenly awoke from a sound sleep to a loud retching sound. I looked at the clock and it was two a.m. Keith wasn't in bed; he was puking his guts out in the bathroom. Deathly ill with excruciating stomach pains and nausea, he had no control over his bowels or vomiting. I couldn't imagine what was wrong with him. Then just a few minutes later the same syndrome overtook me; first nausea and acute stomach pains, then vomiting and diarrhea. The two of us violently erupting from both-ends, only one porcelain-throne and one plastic waste basket between us, we were a horrendous sight. After a few interminable hours of purging every fluid in our bodies we both collapsed in bed.

With a ceaseless chain of agonizing stomach spasms and every bone in my body aching, I felt like a train had run over me. Keith was suffering the same debilitating symptoms. The only common denominator in the equation was the prawns; we clearly had food poisoning.

A devastating hurricane had hit the Hawaiian Islands just days before we'd arrived. The raging storm had ravaged Kauai. The island of Oahu suffered very little damage, mainly widespread power outages. Without the restaurant's knowledge they'd probably lost power, consequently serving us contaminated seafood. We were anxious to call them but it was very early in the morning and they weren't open yet.

I waited a few hours, and then mustered up enough energy to lift the receiver and make the call. I spoke to the manager and asked him if he'd received any other complaints. Unwilling to take responsibility for poisoning us he played dumb and flat out denied it. Without any leftover food samples we had no way to prove our allegation.

As we both lay there moaning and feeling like we were one step from death's door we agreed that neither of us could recover fast enough to enjoy our brief stay in Honolulu. I commented to Keith that I hoped this wasn't a bad omen. I was only kidding of course and though it hurt to do so we both laughed.

After three days we both felt much better. Sorry to have missed the Honolulu experience we still had plenty to look forward to on the next two islands.

Our second stop was the big island of Hawaii. We visited the black sand beach and drove all the way up to the top of Chain of Volcano Drive. The island was magnificently beautiful and lush. I couldn't believe that exotic Anthuriums grew wild along the roadside. We took a cliff-side drive to the other side of the island with the Pacific Ocean below us on our right and countless waterfalls cascading down the mountainside on the left. The picturesque scenery took our breath away.

The last leg of our honeymoon vacation was spent in Maui. We stayed at the finest hotel/resort in Lahaina at that time, the Hyatt Maui. Every hotel room provided panoramic views of mountains, the half-acre pool, the Kaanapal beach, and the Pacific Ocean. Although we touched on the highlights of the island we especially took advantage of the relaxation our hotel had to offer. Laid back Maui was the perfect place to conclude our unforgettable dream vacation.

Twenty-Four: Dollhouse

The price of anything is the amount of life you exchange for it.
~ Henry David Thoreau

When we came back to Baltimore we began our everyday life as newlyweds. As far as I could tell Keith was still keeping his sobriety in check. He had stopped going to N.A. meetings and had an occasional drink, but all things considered I thought he was doing very well. I continued working my part-time office job and Keith resumed his usual work schedule.

I couldn't look at the dilapidated bachelor pad anymore. Keith's parents generously offered to buy us furniture and pay to remodel the kitchen. The house would finally get the woman's touch it needed. I consulted with a kitchen remodeling company and then engaged them to design the layout. They expertly utilized every inch of the small space. The renovation itself was messy and inconvenient but worth it. In the end I had a beautiful, custom-designed kitchen with lots more cabinet space.

I moved our bedroom from the odd-shaped room downstairs to an upstairs dormer. My sister had given us a beautiful bed set as a wedding present. I bought coordinating fabric and transformed the hard, ugly brown headboard into a pretty padded one. Then I matched wallpaper to the headboard and had new carpeting installed. After removing the outlandish shag carpeting from the walls the mutilated wallboard was replaced and painted. A cozy little sanctum rose from the ruins.

I turned the downstairs bedroom into a softly colored, comfy den that became our favorite room of the house. A glass company removed the hideous gold marbleized mirror squares in the living room and then recovered the entire wall with a solid mirror. The expansive reflection added significant dimension and depth to the small-scaled room.
I ordered a cheerful, modern sectional sofa with lots of loose pillows and an oriental-style brass coffee table for the living room. We sold the homely brown sofa and put the old busted up coffee table out to pasture. The entire interior got a fresh coat of paint or wallpaper and new window blinds. The stale outdated bachelor-pad gradually morphed into an adorable little dollhouse. The house still had its share of age related issues, but I'd given it my signature style and it finally felt like home.

Now that our marriage was official I assumed Keith would add my name to the title of the house. It was only when I brought up the topic that he divulged the fact that he had no intention of sharing ownership with me. Did he not trust me or was it that he didn't have faith in the success of our marriage, I wondered? I aggressively pleaded my case, even resorted to tears, but he would not budge. His word was final... end of discussion. I tried not to dwell on my disappointment, hoping that in time his feelings would change. Anyway, though the house wasn't legally mine I still had carte blanche to improve it however I saw fit.

Keith showed his generosity in other ways. Not long after we were married he bought me a new car. I'd still been driving the 1969 Pontiac Lemans my parents had given me. It ran well but was fourteen years old. I picked out a luxurious white Pontiac Grand Prix Brougham Coupe and then customized it with all the bells and whistles. Gorgeous with its cushy dark-blue velvet upholstery and moon-roof, it looked just like a Cadillac Eldorado. I felt like a million bucks driving that spiffy automobile.

We decided to hold on to the Lemans. With low mileage and in beautiful condition it would eventually be a collector's car. Keith drove it to the produce stand and parked it in the back of their private property. We didn't have a garage at our house so that seemed like the safest place to keep it.

Two months after we moved the Lemans to her resting-place, the Parkville Police Department called to tell me that they'd found my Lemans abandoned on a residential side street. They said that it would be towed if I didn't come and move it.

I couldn't imagine what had happened. Keith and I grabbed the keys and drove his car to the location of the vehicle. Sure enough there she was in all her loveliness parked on the side of the street. The thief had only driven her a few blocks before ditching her. With keys in hand, Keith got out of his car saying he would drive her back to the produce stand. I said that I'd follow him.

I watched him walk over, unlock the driver-side door, and open it. Then he motioned with his hand for me to come to him. We both stood aghast as we peered into the empty car. The scoundrel had stolen all her seats! Imagine trying to drive a car with no seats!

We could do only one thing with the mutilated old girl, call a tow truck and send her to that big parking lot in the sky. We waved a final sad good-bye to her as the truck carried her gutted remains away.

Twenty-Five: It's Always Something

In the book of life, the answers aren't in the back.
~ Charlie Brown

I had assumed that life with "Sober Keith" meant life devoid of drama, but that wasn't exactly true. It was one thing after another. I could always count on something to rear its ugly head and elevate my stress level. I guess you could say that my life was predictably unpredictable. Though I hated all the problems, I was unaware of how much I thrived in that environment.

There was something called a "French drain" around the entire perimeter of our basement floor. It was a three or four inch wide trench between the cinder block walls and the concrete foundation. Its intended function was to prevent the basement from flooding. I suppose in theory the "French drain" performed its function, even though I never understood how an open pit around the basement floor could be good for anything. And I had always related the word "French" to mean something polished and sophisticated, not something as rudimentary as an open gutter. Perhaps the antiquated drain had even served the house well for many years. But by the time I arrived it had become clogged and sluggish like an old man's bowels. I wish that I had known.

My odds and ends including all my sentimental keepsakes had been neatly packed away in boxes on the basement floor. Did it ever occur to me that the basement might flood? I guess not because if it had dawned on me I would have thought to put the boxes up on tables or shelves. It rained like it did in biblical times, the drain backed up, and I lost everything that had been down there. All my treasured cards, letters, yearbooks and memory books, along with a miscellany of other things were unsalvageable, gone forever. I still mourn for the loss of those memories.

Then there was another snow storm saga...

It began to snow early one evening while Keith was driving home from work. He walked in the door holding a zippered bank bag with the days' receipts, then went straight back to the den to place it on the coffee table. The news forecast predicted a significant snow accumulation. I thought it would be wise to make a grocery run before being holed up for any length of time. The truth of the matter was that I didn't want to be stuck in the house without cookies! I asked Keith to drive me to the nearby Giant Supermarket to quickly pick up a few things. We bundled up, locked up the house, and drove the quarter mile stretch to the food store. We were there and back within thirty minutes.

The dogs enthusiastically greeted us when we came home. Dusted from head to toe with snow we dropped our damp jackets on the floor, kicked off our shoes, and headed to the kitchen with our packages. I noticed the mat at the back door askew so I bent down to straighten it. When I moved the mat I discovered a mass of shattered glass that had been inconspicuously swept underneath. Keith came over to figure out what had happened and found the deadbolt unlocked. On the opposite side of the door we saw that the glass on the windowpane, right over the deadbolt key, was broken. The closed mini-blind had concealed the evidence.

Everything else looked exactly the way we'd left it. I'd left the house without my purse and it hadn't been stolen or ransacked. My jewelry hadn't been touched either. In very little time the thieves had executed their plan neatly and with precision, stealing only one thing-- the bank-bag with all the cash. Keith rarely brought cash home from work so that would not have been predictable if anyone had been watching him.

The robbery had been way too coincidental to be a random act, too well planned out to be spontaneous. It looked like a set-up. His father didn't buy the story at all; every road pointed to Keith's involvement though he denied it, hurt that he was under suspicion. Dutifully I defended him to the hilt. To this day the unsolved crime remains a mystery.

And speaking of criminal behavior, one of my greatest fears was realized. I found out only two weeks before it was to happen that his brother Mike would be released from prison.

Sometimes the imagination can blow things way out of proportion. I prayed that this was one of those times. To make matters worse, Keith wanted Mike to live with us for awhile. The thought of being alone in the house with that degenerate thug consumed me; I had no idea what he was capable of. Keith felt sorry for his brother since he had nowhere else to go. I told him I could not tolerate having an ex-con living in our house. Besides, I had worked so hard to keep Keith off of drugs and away from temptation; I was worried about Mike compromising Keith's sobriety. But Keith promised that his brother's stay would be very temporary, only long enough to get himself together and find his own place. He said that my in-laws would take over after that.

Keith knew how to appeal to my empathetic nature. He'd mastered the art of wearing me down. By and by I reluctantly consented to transient lodging for my so-called brother-in-law.

For the most part Mike's stay was unremarkable. I had nothing to be afraid of; he was merely a puffed-up little coward who needed to impress everyone. I saw right through him.

One night the three of us drove to a video rental store looking for a movie to watch. As Keith and I stood facing the shelf of rental tapes, Mike tapped me on the shoulder. He motioned for me to turn around and look at a blonde haired teenage boy standing on the other side of the store. Once he had my attention, he started making kissing noises and thrusting his hips in the direction of the boy, trying to impress me with his "badass" prison behavior. Fortunately the boy didn't notice the obscene gestures directed at him. Knowing that he wanted to get a rise out of me I purposely didn't react, though I found his behavior utterly repulsive. That mostly sums up the kind of creep I was dealing with.

Keith really worked hard at finding his brother a new place. In less than a month we were rid of that sorry sack of crap. My father-in-law gave him a job at the produce stand and Keith saw him every day. At least for the time being he was out of my hair.

Twenty-Six: The Grand Prix Meets the Bus

> *If you can find a path with no obstacles, it probably doesn't lead anywhere.*
> *~ Frank A. Clark*

My mother-in-law extended an invitation for my mother and me to come to Boca and stay in her spare condo. My in-laws lived in a villa apartment on the grounds of the Boca Raton Hotel. They had also recently purchased an oceanfront condo in a luxurious high rise building right on the Boca beach.

For the first time ever, my mom and I went on vacation together. We were so excited. Once in Boca we were treated royally; my in-laws knew no other way. Our days were spent sunning and lunching at The Beach Club. We were treated to a lovely meal every night at a different restaurant.

On the third evening of our trip my father-in-law's sister and brother-in-law joined us at an Italian restaurant for dinner. The six of us were sitting at a round table eating, drinking, and having a great time. I was seated between my mother and my mother-in-law.

My mother-in-law, who'd already had too much to drink, started talking to me about how much she loved living in Florida. I commented that I loved

Florida too and hoped to live there someday. Suddenly she snapped. She began yelling so loudly at me that everyone in the restaurant turned to look at us. She lectured at the top of her voice, "Your place is at home in Baltimore with your husband, not here in Florida. He's got a business to run there and that's your home!"

I was so humiliated. I burst into tears and ran out of the restaurant; my mother followed me out the door. I found the nearest payphone so I could call Keith to tell him what had just happened.

He listened to me rant and comforted me. Then he said that he was sorry but he had some bad news to tell me. I stopped crying and I also stopped breathing. He said that he'd been driving my new Grand Prix and had gotten into an accident with a mass transit bus. He was fine but my car had suffered severe body damage.

*What the f... was **wrong** with him?* I couldn't think of any reason he'd have to drive my car. It was like déjà vu all over again. I didn't know whether to rip into him or just break down and cry. I had pampered that beautiful car. He drove it once and wrecked it.

It was always something. The fact that he wasn't hurt was a good thing but... HE HAD JUST WRECKED MY BRAND NEW CAR! I found it hard to forgive him. My vacation was ruined. *For crying out loud, would the problems **ever** cease?*

He said that my car had been towed to our friend Bruce's car repair body shop. Supposedly the repair would take three or four weeks. I found some consolation in believing that we'd get preferential treatment from Bruce. There was nothing I could do from Florida; I'd be home in two days. Keith swore that in a few weeks my car would be good as new. I trusted him, don't ask me why. I think I had more faith that Bruce wouldn't let me down. That was a better bet.

Three weeks went by, then four, but the car wasn't ready as promised. Bruce told me that the insurance settlement was taking longer than expected so he hadn't been able to order all the parts. With every week that passed I got angrier and more frustrated. Keith kept asking me to be patient. He said he'd "handle" everything.

Two months went by, then three, then four and still no car. Keith said he couldn't imagine why it was taking so long. I had gotten absolutely nowhere with Keith at the helm. It was time for me to take control of the situation...and I was going to give Bruce a piece of my mind!

I surprised him with an impromptu visit to his body shop and asked him to step out outside. Bruce remained disturbingly unflappable as he listened to my unladylike lambasting. He calmly waited for me to finish then said with a smirk, "I'm not the person you should be angry with. If you want to be angry with anyone it should be your husband."

"What the hell are you talking about?" I asked taken aback by his comment.

"Keith took the entire insurance settlement and cashed it in. I don't have enough money to finish fixing your car."

I was dumbfounded. I felt so foolish for my behavior. But I was dealing with two scoundrels. I'd never get the whole truth from either one of them; they were obviously in cahoots. All I wanted was my new car back in its original condition. And come hell or high water, Keith had better make that happen.

I called Keith and ripped into him like a rabid Pit bull. He admitted to taking some of the insurance money but claimed we needed it to pay bills. Besides, he said he'd given our friend more than enough to fix the car. He suggested that Bruce had put it "all up his nose," which I knew was a realistic possibility.

I couldn't believe either one of those consummate liars; they had both been trying to play me. But I shoved a cattle prod so far up their *tuchises*, they couldn't wait to get rid of me! And what do you know...within two weeks I had my car back! The car looked as good as new though unfortunately some of my favorite bells and whistles never worked again.

Twenty-Seven: Fixing Up the Basement

*A man always has two reasons for what he does –
a good one, and the real one.*

~ J.P. Morgan

I know...any women in her right mind would have run from that marriage screaming. The thought that kept replaying in my head was that marriage was a difficult undertaking. I still had hope that it would get better with persistence and time. Call me crazy (because by that point I was), but if it took a lifetime I was determined to make that marriage work. Love would conquer all. Unless it killed me first, I'd find a way to fix him. I'd just have to figure out how.

I was twenty-five years old, Keith was twenty-eight. Maternal feelings were beginning to stir inside of me. Keith had always wanted children; all I had to do was say the word. Obviously I had serious reservations about the stability of my husband's sobriety. Keith swore on his life that he'd never compromise the health or wellbeing of his child. And I also had legitimate concerns about the effect of the father's drug abuse on a developing fetus. I searched but found no evidence suggesting that any previously used drugs in the father's system passed on to his unborn child.

Jewish people of *Ashkenazi* descent have a higher risk of carrying Tay-Sachs, a fatal disease that damages nerve and brain cells, and passing it on to their child. If both parents are carriers there is a chance that any child they have will be born with the disease. Keith and I scheduled an appointment to have our blood drawn at the testing center to rule out the possibility that we were carriers.

I volunteered to go first at the lab. Keith sat in the room with me while the tech drew my blood. When it was his turn he asked me to wait outside the room. I was confused by his request, but he said he'd explain later.

As we were leaving he apologized and explained that after having shot up for so many years several of his veins had collapsed, especially the ones in his arms. The most accessible veins to draw blood from were in his ankles. He said he was embarrassed; he didn't want me to have to see the nurse doing that. In actuality he probably had fresh track marks that would have alerted me to the fact that he was still using. But at the time that never crossed my mind. I wanted to believe that he was straight.

When we received the test results a few days later we were relieved to find out that neither of us carried the gene. With that concern out of the way we began trying to conceive a baby.

Month after month we hoped for my pregnancy but ended up disappointed. After six months of trying I consulted my OB/GYN who assured me that I was healthy. He said it could take up to a year to conceive and we'd look into the problem should that not happen.

After trying unsuccessfully for eleven months I purchased a Basal Thermometer which is used to track a woman's ovulation cycle. The body temperature rises during a woman's most fertile time of the month. If conception doesn't occur, her temperature drops back down until her next ovulation. Knowing that I'd have to chart my temperatures every morning for the next six months I figured that I'd better get a jump start.

I charted my temperature for a few mornings and saw a noticeable rise which indicated that I was fertile. But after seven days my temperature didn't drop back down...and my boobs started burning like towering infernos. I called my doctor and he ordered a blood test. The results came back positive. I was pregnant! The baby was due early in June.

During the first few weeks of my pregnancy I felt great. I hadn't suffered from any morning sickness. Then right between my third and fourth weeks I was besieged by the worst nausea I'd ever experienced. The sick feeling never eased up. I was ill twenty four/seven but with no vomiting. No matter what I tried I couldn't get any relief; I even felt sick in my sleep.

On its own that sensation was enough to incapacitate me. Then a disabling fatigue overtook me; I couldn't lift my head up off the pillow. I lay in bed day in and day out moaning and bargaining with God. My sense of smell had dramatically heightened; subtle odors I'd never noticed before now turned me green. Each day when Keith came home from work I could literally smell the vegetables he'd trimmed up that day. I also knew by his smell what stores he had delivered produce to. And because he was a heavy cigarette smoker, the smoky odor that clung to him smelled even more putrid than normal, and made me gag.

When he'd get home from work he'd come right upstairs to kiss me hello. I'd holler, "You trimmed up celery today didn't you? Get away from me, you're making me gag! You know you're supposed to shower after you've trimmed up celery!" I wish I could say that I was exaggerating about the severity of my nausea but I'm not. He might as well have rolled in Eau De Dog Poop! It all smelled the same to me.

I'd never imagined that my first trimester would cause me so much suffering. My doctor assured me that my symptoms indicated a healthy pregnancy, so I dealt with the torture one day at a time. Each day I hoped that tomorrow would be better and tried to focus on the prize at the end. Magically in my fourteenth week the symptoms disappeared. Suddenly I felt great! Food smelled and tasted good again, and I was always hungry.

Every evening I'd section a grapefruit, and with the bowl resting on my stomach I'd eat it while I watched television in bed. I'd heard that eating grapefruit helped to ease fluid retention. One evening I rested the bowl on my stomach and it began to jump. At first I couldn't figure out what was happening, and then it dawned on me that the baby was kicking it! I had never been aware of any movement before. I yelled for Keith to come upstairs and then proudly showed him the jumping bowl. We were elated.

Keith had tried his best to stay downstairs most of the time while I was sick to avoid aggravating my symptoms. Using the spare time to his benefit he'd fixed up the front part of the basement and turned it into a usable den. He put a television set down there and began spending lots of time in his "man-cave." Once I was up and about he proudly showed off the fruits of his labor. It seemed as if his impending fatherhood had given him a new lease on life. I had never seen him so ambitious.

Keith was so excited about having a baby. He'd dreamed about it for as long as he could remember. He sang funny songs to my belly so the baby would know his voice. I didn't want to know the sex of the baby ahead of time, and Keith had no reason to find out since he knew we were having a girl. He'd already chosen Cammy as the girl's name. I loved the name too, but only as her nickname. We had a much harder time deciding on a boy's name... just in case.

While upstairs and confined to bed I'd been completely consumed with how bad I felt. I had given up my watch post; I hadn't realized how much time Keith had been spending in the basement with his brother. When I was finally up and about, I began to notice how often Mike was at our house. Whenever he'd come over the two of them would go right down to the basement to "hang out and watch TV." I told Keith I didn't like his brother coming over so often. He said Mike was lonely and badly needed the friendship. I knew nothing positive could come from their camaraderie.

I began to notice some unusual occurrences with Keith. Every time I called him at work he was out delivering produce orders and would be gone for unusually long periods of time. He was giving me less and less money to cover our bills, and he kept losing his house keys. I reverted back to panic mode.

One Saturday afternoon, with my permission, Keith borrowed my Grand Prix to run an errand. He said he'd be extra careful and promised he'd bring it back with a full tank of gas.

As the proverb goes, "There are none so blind as those who will not see."

Before an hour had even passed the telephone in our house rang. I answered it and a Baltimore County Police Officer asked me with whom he was speaking. Once I had identified myself he went on to explain that his partner and he were patrolling the Sudbrook Middle School area when they noticed a suspicious looking car in an otherwise vacant parking lot. When they approached the car they saw a man in the driver's seat with a hypodermic needle in his arm. The man had no identification but told the officer his name and explained that his wife was the owner of the car.

The officer told me they were going to charge my husband with possession of Cocaine, drug paraphernalia, and driving with a revoked license. I said I'd be right there. I have to admit, after everything I'd gone through with Keith I wasn't as concerned for his wellbeing as I was for my car.

The last time Keith had been charged with a DUI the judge had found him guilty and revoked his license. That never stopped him from driving though. Apparently he thought that he was above the law. This time I was tempted to tell the officer to cart him away to jail. But there was a lot at stake in my life and that would have only complicated the mess.

When I arrived on the scene my Grand Prix was parked in the empty lot facing the road with the driver's-side door wide open. The police cruiser was parked next to it and two officers were leaning on my car. My mind flashed right back to the night of the downtown incident. My glassy-eyed, stupefied husband peered up at me from the driver's seat and tried to tell me something but his words came out like muddleheaded blubber. I think he was trying to apologize to me.

The officers showed me the drugs and drug paraphernalia that they'd confiscated from my car. They handed me a court citation and gave me the option of either having them arrest him or accepting his release to my custody. Believing that it was better for both of us if I took charge of the situation, I dispassionately agreed to take him home. I didn't need him sitting in jail; we were going to have a baby and I had to whip him into shape in a hurry.

Twenty-Eight: The Resident Coconut

Optimism is a cheerful frame of mind that enables a tea kettle to sing though it's in hot water up to its nose.
~ Author Unknown

Keith was in the perilous throes of his most deadly addiction ever; main-lined Cocaine. Each day his irrepressible compulsion lured him to menacing places infested with cesspools of humanity.

He continued his daily routine of getting up in the morning and going to work. But every afternoon he'd leave the produce market under the guise of making deliveries and head downtown to cop drugs. He often found himself on the wrong side of the barrel of some hoodlum's gun. It's hard to believe that he never got shot or killed. After completing the drug deal he'd get back in his pickup truck, shoot up, then nod out on the steering wheel for a couple of hours. When he woke up from his stupor he'd go back to work as if nothing had ever happened. Then he'd come home to me at the usual time.

During the weeks and months that all this was happening I wasn't privy to those worrisome details. He was still trying his best to hide his dirty little secret from both his father and me. I learned all the disturbing facts later on.

Even before I knew all the details, it was obvious to me that Keith was in terrible shape. The car incident was the first red flag, and then I started noticing other odd things. A mature sounding African American woman named "Miss so and so" called the house looking for him one day. Based on the questions she asked me I had no doubt that her call was drug related.

Keith began losing his house keys on a semi-daily basis. It worried me to think about those sewer rats having our telephone number and quite possibly the keys to our home. I couldn't believe that with my pregnancy and after everything I'd done for him he would put me through this.

I felt stupid. I blamed myself for not watching him. Now it was almost too late; things had come to a head. I had one last chance to save him for the sake of the baby and the future of our family.

I scheduled an emergency appointment for the two of us to see his addiction therapist. It had been months since his last counseling session. This crisis had reached desperate proportions; if he didn't get to inpatient treatment right away he was going to die or end up in jail. My safety and wellbeing were seriously at risk as well. I prayed that his therapist would be successful in persuading him to go to rehab.

I was disheartened, though not the least bit surprised, when Keith refused inpatient treatment. He was not going to make this easy for me…then again nothing was ever easy when it came to Keith; he was incredibly stubborn. But the future of our family hinged on his getting well. As a codependent and diehard enabler I'd spent most of our relationship covering up for his "slips." It had been a weighty, exhaustive burden that

I'd voluntarily assumed, but I could no longer handle the wanton problem alone. In order to force him into treatment he'd have to be hit where it hurt him the most. Work was his Achilles heel.

The only person who could possibly help me in that endeavor was his father. Keith's father adored him; he wanted so badly to believe in his son. But after the torment Keith had put his parents through over the years, his father's wounds ran deep and his ability to trust was fragile. I had protected him from the truth; the news of his son's decline would surely devastate him. I expected the disclosure to release a loud, angry tirade. That was how my father-in-law expressed himself. But behind the rage was an abundance of love. I'd just have to face the music.

I braced myself for the pent-up anger and hollow threats about to be unleashed in my direction. That was going to be hard to take. But I knew that no matter what Keith did, his father would not give up on him. With full awareness that the shit was about to hit the fan, I made the telephone call.

Since Keith had gone through inpatient rehab before, his father questioned why I thought it would work this time. I suggested that his dream of becoming a father could provide a powerful motivation to get and stay straight. I convinced him that for the baby's sake we had to give rehabilitation a try. It was our only option. He agreed and asked how he could help. I told him to confront Keith about his Cocaine addiction, telling him in no uncertain terms that he was banned from work until he admitted himself into treatment and got clean. My father-in-law was more than willing to take my direction.

When confronted by his father Keith did the only thing he knew how to do; he lied about his addiction. But my father-in-law didn't buy into his excuses, so Keith pleaded his case and begged for compassion. That didn't work either so he began negotiating. He employed all of his usual manipulation tactics but his father wouldn't budge. Keith was backed into a corner; he had no choice but to finally concede. He agreed to go to treatment.

I called his therapist right away to give him the update. He said he would send Keith to a rehab facility called The Terraces in Lancaster, Pennsylvania, an hour and a half drive from our home. As soon as we hung up the phone he made all the arrangements.

I was so relieved that Keith finally agreed to go. I thought all my problems were over, but they weren't...I still had to physically get him there. And his therapist explained that after the intake process, most addicts go into panic mode because they're cut off from their drugs. He warned me that Keith would probably call me the first night, tug at my heartstrings, and try to convince me to take him home. I'd have to be strong and my resolve impervious.

Keith's father drove him to Lancaster, and to my great relief he checked himself into The Terraces according to the plan.

As his therapist had predicted, he called me the first night crying and pleading with me to come get him. He referred to the facility as a dump and claimed that they were treating him abusively. He knew exactly how to push my buttons and he succeeded in upsetting me. But I didn't let on that he'd gotten to me; nothing he said could ever have convinced me to rescue him. I told him that it wasn't going to be easy but that he'd just have to deal with it.

It wasn't going to be a picnic for me either. Sadly, I would spend the sixth month of my pregnancy all alone. I resented him for that. But I looked forward to the peace and quiet. I desperately needed rest.

As per my request, before Keith left he had hired a contractor to build a badly needed closet in the dormer nursery upstairs. He gave the carpenter a couple hundred dollars to buy materials and to get started. I'd pay him the balance upon his completion of the job. What I didn't know but soon discovered was that the carpenter was one of Keith's drug cohorts. And that shifty maggot would be alone with me in our house, fully aware that my husband was out of the picture for the entire month.

Using the money Keith had given him he bought some lumber then brought it to our house and haphazardly dumped it in the first floor hallway. The first day after working for just a few hours he asked me for money to buy more supplies. That wasn't the original deal but he convinced me to give him fifty dollars anyway. Then he left for the day. Wood scraps and screws remained wherever he'd dropped them. The house was a dusty, filthy mess. That really irked me, but I figured I'd put up with it for a few days until he finished the job.

I realized whom and what I was dealing with when the bum tried to hit me up for more cash on the second day. The guy thought he had sized me up as an easy mark but he was wrong. I told him that I'd have to discuss the money issue with Keith first. Truthfully I didn't want him ever stepping foot in my house again, though I worried about my safety if I fired him. My nerves were frazzled. Keith had gone away and left me with yet another mess to deal with, literally and figuratively.

The guy showed up one more time complaining that he couldn't finish the job without more money. Once he realized that he wasn't getting anymore cash from me he left and never returned. But his carelessly scattered heaps of rubble remained. A cumbersome pile of lumber that was too heavy for me to move by myself obstructed the entire first floor hallway.

Eventually a reputable carpenter of my choosing took over the job, completed the project in a few days, and left the house immaculate. I was so relieved. But I still couldn't rest.

The Terraces strongly encouraged the participation of families as part of their therapy program. They felt it was an integral part of the addict's rehabilitation. The family program involved a one-week stay at the facility with room and board provided.

So, seven months pregnant, in the dead of the winter of 1985, I drove to Lancaster and checked myself in for the week. Everything I brought with me had to be inspected to ensure that I wasn't smuggling any contraband into the facility. They even took apart my hairdryer and searched inside. Though I understood the need for tight security, I still found the intake process demeaning.

The Terraces was a defunct hotel that had been purchased and turned into a drug rehab center. The layout of the building remained the same as it did in the original hotel. The suites each had two double beds and their own private bathroom. Whether inpatient or family member, everyone had to share their room with a roommate. I was paired with the mother of another addict. During the week of my visit all the other family members staying there were parents. I was the only spouse and definitely the only pregnant woman.

Because addicts by nature are chronic habitual users, when they avoid one substance they usually substitute something else. Many substance abusers smoke cigarettes to fill that void. Cigarettes were never a substitute for Keith; he'd already been a chain smoker for years. And after a week of breathing in the smoked filled air at The Terraces, I think I inadvertently inhaled an entire pack myself.

The patient treatment plans varied based on the type of drug abused. Keith was grouped with the Cocaine addicts, good-humoredly referred to as "The Coconuts." The family members were all grouped together, and the substance abusers participated along with us in some of our workshops. The week was emotionally challenging and intensely introspective. The counselors worked us hard; we had papers to write and homework assignments every night. By the end of the week I was totally exhausted and more than anxious to go home.

Keith had one more week to go; he was counting the minutes. I planned to pick him up on the morning of his release then we'd drive to Philadelphia for a romantic weekend. We missed being together and that would give us both something to look forward to.

That year the eastern U.S. was in the grips of one of the harshest cold waves ever. All-time record lows were set in Baltimore at a numbing minus seven degrees. Weather-wise, February was always an unpredictable month.

I awoke to a snowy blizzard on the morning of Keith's discharge day. Judging by the substantial accumulation and sizeable snowdrifts I could tell that the blustery storm had been raging all night. The roads in front and on the side of our house were thickly blanketed with unspoiled virgin snow, indicating that a snowplow had yet to come. Main arteries and highways were usually attended to before residential side streets.

As much as I hated to disappoint Keith, under those conditions I didn't see how I could drive to Lancaster. I was fairly skilled at handling a car on snowy roads, but even if our street was plowed and I dug my car out, the chance remained that someone would slide into me. That would be risky for anyone, but especially for a woman in her third trimester of pregnancy. Surely my safety and the safety of his unborn child would override Keith's eagerness for liberation.

Oblivious to the weather conditions, Keith called home at nine o'clock that morning asking what time I'd be picking him up. I explained the problem, fully expecting he'd insist I stay home. But instead of selfless resignation he ranted and raved. He wanted me there come hell or high water. I understood what was driving his anger, but I couldn't believe his lack of consideration for my welfare. Still I felt sorry for him. I told him to call me back in an hour; I'd see what I could do. I hung up the phone and called my father for advice, knowing he'd have my best interest at heart.

I'd never known my father to be intimidated by "a little snow." He didn't think the main roads or highways would be nearly as hazardous as the side streets appeared to be. He offered to drive to Lancaster and bring Keith home. I appreciated his offer; at least I had a viable option. The only drawback would be forfeiting our weekend together in Philly.

I opened the front door and looked outside. The snow had stopped falling and a few neighbors were outside shoveling their walks and clearing off their cars. It hadn't snowed in Lancaster or Philadelphia and they weren't in the path of the storm. I called my father back to ask how he felt about me driving there alone. He said that once I reached the highway I shouldn't have any problem. He offered to come over and clean off my car. When Keith called me back I had good news for him. I'd be there by noon.

Twenty-Nine: The Thirteenth Step

Sometimes, perhaps, we are allowed to get lost that we may find the right person to ask directions of.
~ Robert Brault

Our weekend together in Philadelphia was the perfect way for us to transition back into our married life after a month of being apart. Keith had so much to share about his experiences at The Terraces and the friends he'd made while he was there. He finally opened up to me about his Cocaine addiction; how it began and the calamitous influence it'd had over him. He described the hellish places his addiction had driven him to and the torment he suffered knowing how much he was hurting me.

We shared our hopes and dreams for our baby. While dazed under the hypnotic influence of his addiction, he had previously disregarded my pregnancy. Now lucid, he beamed with excitement for his impending fatherhood. He hadn't wavered in his certainty that we were having a girl. I never admitted it but I thought I was carrying a girl too. Every mother says she doesn't care what sex her baby is as long as it's healthy. That was absolutely my number one concern...but if I had one more wish I wanted a daughter.

I knew better than to ask about his sobriety, and he wasn't falsely promising the permanence of it. His life would be a perpetual uphill climb. Whether or not he could withstand the pressure, no one could say. And if wishes would make it so, he'd never use again. I desperately wanted to save my marriage and to provide a stable, emotionally healthy, two-parent home for our child. He'd been handed all the tools and provided all the resources he needed to stay clean. But it went without saying that the only promise he could make to himself and to me was to face his addiction one day at a time.

The next step for Keith was his full immersion in the Narcotics Anonymous Twelve Step Program. He had to find a sponsor as soon as possible and attend N.A. meetings at least once a day for an undeterminable amount of time. Without constant support he'd never survive.

Keith attended his N.A. meetings daily. As recommended, he severed all associations with other addicts not in a twelve-step program. His diabolical brother headed up that list. I knew he constantly struggled with drug cravings but still he seemed reasonably happy. The impending birth of our baby gave him a goal to focus on. He managed his life one day at a time and I tried my best not to worry.

I needed the support that The Nar-Anon Family Group offered. They help those who are experiencing desperation due to the addiction problem of someone close to them. Keith's addiction had become my addiction. I lived my life on the edge, scrutinizing his words and actions, wondering when my life would crumble again. I'd allowed him to define my happiness and control every aspect of my life. Living that way didn't help him and it was destroying me. He'd either sink or swim but I had to get well for the sake of my baby.

I never imagined I'd find myself participating in a twelve-step program. I pictured a group of spiritually wounded individuals sitting around telling their tales of woe. That mental image put me off even though I'd heard that people greatly benefited from those programs. With apprehension, but leaving all judgment aside, I courageously walked into an afternoon meeting that was being held at a nearby church.

As I entered the room, each person warmly greeted me, introducing him or herself by first name only. When everyone was seated, the meeting began with The Serenity prayer said in unison. Then the chairwoman leading the meeting asked if anyone would like to "share." I'd never heard the word "share" used in that context before. I thought it sounded so much nicer than saying, "Who wants to complain to us about their life?" The first person sharing stated their first name and the entire group responded, "Hi (name of the person)," in unison. After the person had spoken, the group as a whole said, "Thanks for sharing. Keep coming back." No one offered advice, no one judged.

Feeling surprisingly comfortable for my first visit, I chose to share next. Following their lead, I stated my first name, my reason for attendance, and highlights (or lowlights if you will) of life with my addict. I felt the group's warmth and compassion as they patiently listened to my sad account. Patiently is the operable word; with the exception of minor details, the essences of all our stories were the same.

One regular to the group was the wife of a recovering addict who'd been sober for many years. Still, she never missed a meeting. All the other regulars were parents of actively using addicts.

I opened the Nar-Anon handbook that the meeting chairwoman handed to me and silently read the first three steps of the Nar-Anon twelve-step program. They were stated as follows:

1. We admitted we were powerless over the Addict -- that our lives had become unmanageable.
2. Came to believe that a Power greater than ourselves could restore us to sanity.
3. Made a decision to turn our will and our lives over to the care of God as we *understood* Him.

I had no problem understanding the first step-- admitting that I was powerless. That's why I was there in the first place. But the second and third steps gave me pause. Yes, I was raised in an observant Jewish home, but I personally had no faith in God or any "power greater than myself." Truthfully, I found the whole God concept far-fetched. I found God's portrayal wrathful and intimidating; he seemed foreboding and untouchable. Judaism as it had been presented to me as a child and young adult, never impacted me spiritually or nurtured my soul. I resented having to blindly follow rules that I didn't understand, didn't believe in, or that made no sense to me. I've always been a logical thinker.

So for me, the hardest part of initiating the steps was to figure out who or what to turn my problems and my pain over to. I struggled to find a source of strength outside of myself to trust in.

The Nar-Anon family functions as a support system. The members of the group do not try to solve each other's problems. They only share experiences for the benefit of others. That is why I paid particularly close attention to the words offered to me in private one evening by our chairwoman. She said, "As parents of addicts we are burdened with our problems for the rest of our lives. We have no choice but to accept our situation. You are still young and your whole life is ahead of you. You don't have to try so hard. You can walk away from all of this and move on with your life."

Though unprepared to hear her words, what she said made perfect sense to me. Still I felt I had to defend my position. Questioning my own words as I spoke them, my answer sounded uncertain. "I married him to spend our lives together. I promised to love him for good or bad, in sickness and in health. I'm trying to keep my promise, to stand by him and make our marriage work."

I hoped for affirmation to my reasoning but her response was simple, "Just keep in mind that you don't have to."

Thirty: Birth of an Angel

*Whatever they grow up to be,
they are still our children, and the
one most important of all the
things we can give to them is un-
conditional love. Not a love that
depends on anything at all except
that they are our children.*
~ Rosaleen Dickson

With my due date right around the corner I went into nesting mode. I stayed busy organizing everything I could get my hands on. Besides being sick and bedridden for the first trimester, my pregnancy had gone smoothly. Considering the terrible stress I'd been under for most of my pregnancy it was remarkable that I'd had no complications.

On May 6, 1985 at 5:38 P.M., two weeks and six days before my actual due date, I gave birth by Cesarean section to a five-pound eight-ounce perfect little baby girl. Keith stood by my side, watching the entire surgery and witnessing the joyous birth of our daughter. We named her Cameryn April so she'd have a professional name to use as an adult, but we'd call her Cammy.

After her birth I held my baby just long enough to count her fingers and toes and admire her pretty little ears. Then they whisked her away to the nursery while sending me to recovery. Keith and all four grandparents alternately kept an eye on her in the nursery so I knew she was fine, but I didn't get to see her again for almost twenty-four hours. It upset me that the nurses wouldn't bring her to me sooner. I ached to hold her.

After my C-Section I was required to stay in the hospital for five days. I had the option of having the baby room-in with me and keeping her overnight, or sending her to the nursery so I could sleep. I wanted to do everything for the baby myself. The abdominal incision burned every time I moved, but I resolutely got up to care for her. I allowed them to take her back to the nursery only when the doctors needed to examine her.

On her fourth day she developed infant jaundice. It's a very common condition that is due to the immaturity of the baby's liver. Many babies develop infant jaundice after they have already gone home. In mild cases it often disappears on its own within two or three weeks. Since Cammy's jaundice developed while she was still in the hospital she had to stay for treatment.

Phototherapy, which assists in the excretion of bilirubin, is the method of treatment for infant jaundice. Wearing only a diaper and protective eye patches, the baby is placed under special lights for between twenty-four to forty-eight hours. The baby's eyes are covered to avoid the possibility of retinal damage from exposure to the ultraviolet light. The bilirubin levels are monitored daily through blood samples taken from the bottom of the baby's feet.

Cammy was a breastfed baby so I had to go down to the nursery every three hours to feed her. She looked so cute the first time I saw her sunbathing on her back under the light, wearing only a diaper and her paper "sunglasses." But when I came down in the middle of the night for her next feeding I found her lying on her back without eye protection, staring straight up at the light. She must have pulled the covering off her eyes while the nurse wasn't paying attention. I starting frantically screaming, "My baby's gonna be blind, my baby's gonna be blind! Who's supposed to be watching my baby?"

The nurse on duty hurried over, put the patches back over Cammy's eyes, and told me to calm down. I didn't see any reason why I should calm down. She said that the limited exposure would not damage the baby's eyes. I'd already witnessed her gross negligence so I had no faith in her "professional" opinion. Of course she would say that to cover her own ass. She brazenly told me that I was upsetting all the babies and to please quiet down.

Not wanting to stress out my baby or upset the entire nursery, I forced myself to get a grip. The nurse looked down her nose at me, then picked up Cammy and put her in my arms so I could feed her. When I returned to my room I called my pediatrician and left an urgent message. It was the middle of the night and my message had obviously awoken him. He called me right back, half-asleep, to tell me not to worry. He assured me that he'd examine her eyes later that morning. It turned out she was fine.

To avoid dealing with more hormonal lunacy from this neurotic first-time mother, the nurses did not let that happen again...at least not to my baby. Because of her condition, Cammy had to stay in the hospital two days longer than I did. The doctor offered me the choice of remaining there with her or going home. I refused to leave the hospital without my baby.

I proudly celebrated my very first Mother's Day, Sunday, May 12th, in the hospital. Keith came to visit in the late morning, my parents and in-laws came in the afternoon.

Around eight o'clock that evening, long after my visitors had gone home, my private telephone rang. I picked up the receiver and heard my mother-in-law's voice on the other end. The caustic tone of her voice scared me. Clearly upset and sounding intoxicated, she started off by telling me what a good-for-nothing husband I had. She said that while I lay in the hospital with his baby he was home getting loaded. Too messed up to have gotten his own Mother's Day gift for me, Keith had asked her to buy it and then planned to take all the credit. She told me that, per Keith's instructions, she'd left my gift in a brown paper bag in the back of my closet. Then she abruptly ended the call.

The only two words I uttered the entire time were "Okay" and "Bye." Taken aback, I doubted what I had heard. I questioned her state of mind and her motive for ratting out her son. Then I got up to look in the closet. Sure enough I found the brown paper bag with a bottle of my mother-in-law's favorite perfume in it exactly where she said she'd left it.

Keith would have never picked that gift out for me. I knew she had told me the truth.

Recovering from surgery and exhausted from the demands of a new baby, I didn't have the energy to get into it with Keith. What was the point anyway? I'd heard enough lies, excuses, and empty promises. I just lied there all alone sobbing and forlorn.

And just like that, the joy of my very first Mother's Day along with all my hopes and dreams for our family were shattered. I could no longer kid myself. My husband had an ungovernable, incurable disease that he'd never recover from and there was nothing I could do about it. Though disillusioned, I didn't have the luxury of a prolonged pity-party; I had a baby to take care of. I'd allowed my own suffering but the buck stopped there; Cammy was off limits. I'd protect her with my life.

That same day I'd gotten the good news that Cammy's jaundice disappeared and we could go home the next day. Keith and I had already arranged the plans. The baby couldn't leave the hospital without first being secured in an infant car seat, so Keith had brought it up to my room before he'd left earlier in the day. He said he'd call me first thing on Monday morning for the time of our discharge so he'd know when to pick us up. I couldn't wait to bring my baby home.

The nurse told me early the next morning that we'd be discharged at eleven. Anticipating Keith's call, I quickly showered and dressed in regular clothes for the first time that week. At ten o'clock, with still no word from Keith, I fed the baby, changed her diaper, and dressed her in her new going home outfit. Cammy, barely five-and-a-half pounds seemed miniaturized by the overly large newborn sized outfit. Preemie clothing would have fit much better but there was no such thing at the time.

Getting impatient, I called Keith at home and then at work; I couldn't find him anywhere. I hoped his inaccessibility meant that he was already on his way.

Eleven o'clock came and went but still no Keith. I couldn't imagine how long he expected me to wait knowing how badly I wanted to go home.
Frustrated, I alternated between pacing the floor and sitting in the chair nervously tapping my foot. By the time twelve o'clock rolled around I was seething with anger. I called my father, told him what had happened, and asked him to pick us up. He said that he would leave right away and would be there in about twenty minutes.

Ten minutes later my telephone rang. It was Keith. As if nothing was wrong, he asked what time he should pick us up. I responded icily with two words, "Don't bother." When pressed for an explanation I viciously chewed his head off. He became indignant when I told him my father was already on his way. In his usual defensive bullying tone he declared that he was the father and no one else was going to take his baby home. He ordered me to wait for him because he also was on his way. I was exhausted from everything I'd been through. It didn't matter who picked us up, I just wanted to go home.

My father got there first. He didn't mind at all that Keith was coming and that he wanted me to wait. When Keith arrived, my father happily assisted with escorting Cammy and me out of the hospital, then into the car. I was glad my father came; it was comforting to have him there. Then finally, with the baby securely in her infant car seat, our new little family of three headed home.

Thirty-One: Leaving the Danger Zone

Relationships are like glass. Sometimes it is better to leave them broken then try to hurt yourself putting them back together.

~ Author Unknown

K eith had dreamed Cammy to life down to the very last detail; she was the spitting image of him. If the pride and adoration he had for his daughter couldn't keep him straight then nothing could. But the handwriting was on the wall; I knew that it was only a matter of time before he bottomed out again. With all the demands of having a new baby to care for, I didn't have time to focus on Keith's impending doom.

Cammy slept a great deal the first four weeks of her life. I found it difficult to keep her awake long enough during feedings to sustain her for more than two hours at a time. And if that wasn't frustrating or tiring enough, she seemed intent on restricting my food intake too. Every time I tried to eat something she'd smell the food and wake up from a sound sleep, crying. I wish I could say that she helped me to lose weight but I compensated by rapidly wolfing down whatever I could eat before she caught me.

As the first grandchild on both sides of the family, Cammy had a captive audience. And as first time grandparents, they all took the liberty of overexploiting their bragging rights.

When the baby turned two weeks old she was scheduled for her first visit to the pediatrician. I still couldn't walk the steps or drive while recovering from my surgery so my mother-in-law volunteered her services. Capitalizing on the first opportunity to spoil Cammy, she insisted on driving her to the doctor in the Rolls Royce. From the very beginning, Grandma would see to it that her only granddaughter had nothing but the best.

My parents were overcome with joy over their new grandbaby. In their immodest opinion a more special child had never been born. My father said that the first time he looked into Cammy's eyes he saw a wise, knowing soul; an old soul with intelligence far beyond her few hours on this earth.

Keith seemed to keep his drug habit in check for the first month. We played the "don't ask don't tell" game. But it wasn't long before he began spiraling out of control again.

Keith had begun to show signs of paranoia. When he'd come into the house after work, he'd walk from window to window closing each blind. The bay window in the living room didn't have any blinds so he had used thumbtacks to hang a sheet in front of it. Sometimes he would carry a dining room chair to the front of the house and jam the back of it under the doorknob. I kept noticing him peeking outside, especially whenever the dogs barked.

Though I wasn't sure what would finally push me out the door, I suspected it wouldn't take long. The saddest part was that I was still very much in love with my husband. I couldn't bear the thought of being without him.

I honestly did not know that love wasn't supposed to be painful. I thought that hurt was a positive thing that proved the depth of the love between two people.

In retrospect, I understand that Keith had become my drug of choice. I was addicted to the addict. I thought I needed him in my life to be happy. He wasn't the only one with the problem...I was sick too.

One evening Keith offered to go out and pick up steamed crabs for dinner. We rarely ate them so I looked forward to the special treat. Since he didn't have enough cash in his wallet or any credit cards, he told me he would see if his "friend" would cash a check. The friend he referred to owned a popular Chinese restaurant that was not far from our house. According to Keith, the guy had cashed checks for him before so he didn't think there'd be a problem. He said he'd be right back.

In the meantime I covered the dining room table with newspaper, laid out the knives and mallets, and filled a pitcher of water. Knowing how messy and time consuming picking crabs was, I fed the baby so she'd hopefully sleep while we ate. Then I waited.

Almost two hours went by before Keith finally returned home. As he walked into the den where I was sitting, the savory smell of Old Bay seasoning emanated from the dampened brown paper bag clenched in his hand. He was glassy eyed and stumbling.

I took one look at him and cried, "You're unbelievable!"

He looked confused. With slurred words he said "What do you mean?" Sounding sincerely concerned he continued, "I brought you the crabs?"

I picked up the baby and marched upstairs. Then grabbing the first suitcase I could find hurriedly threw in some clothing and necessities for Cammy and me.

Keith had barely figured out what was happening before I dashed out the door with Cammy in my arms and drove away. I didn't know where I was heading; I just had the compulsion to run.

After driving aimlessly for more than twenty minutes I spotted a familiar hotel off the side of the highway. The adrenaline rush had worn off and I felt weary. I needed a quiet place to gather my thoughts so I exited the highway, drove into the hotel parking lot, and booked a room for the night.

We checked out of the hotel at around six o'clock the next morning. I headed home, expecting Keith to have already left for work; the last thing I wanted was a confrontation. But when I approached the house I could see that his truck was still parked outside. That was highly unusual.

I parked my car around the corner and waited for him to leave. Still after forty-five minutes of waiting, the white pickup truck remained in front of the house. It did not appear that he was going anywhere so I pulled my car around to the front of the house and parked. I couldn't sit in the car all day with the baby.

I had just stepped out of my car when my next door neighbor approached me. She asked if everything was all right. Not wanting to commit to an answer I asked her why she wanted to know. Then she informed me that the police were at my house at nine o'clock the previous night. I told her that I had spent the night away from home so I had no idea what was going on. In actuality the police had showed up at our house several times before but I had been instructed by Keith to never answer the door.

Love or no love, it became clear that I'd have to get the baby and myself out of there as soon as possible. I couldn't bear to think about leaving Shane and Honeybell behind, but from that point on I knew that I would have to make difficult choices. I hoped to eventually find a place for all of us to live, but with no job, no money, and no source of income that wasn't going to be easy. Throwing Keith out of the house wasn't an option. He had never added my name to the title and I finally understood why.

Keith heard me come in the house and met me at the door. He immediately began hurling verbal assaults at me. Refusing to take his crap any longer I got right up in his face and gave it all back to him. The upheaval upset the baby and she started to cry. I told him I had nothing more to say and headed upstairs with Cammy. Keith followed right behind. Once the baby had quieted down, I laid her in the crib and then went in to finish up with Keith, who had been waiting for me in our bedroom. I told him that I could no longer tolerate his addiction; I had nothing more to give. I said I'd be moving out as soon as I found somewhere for Cammy and me to live.

He cried and pleaded with me to give him another chance, but I told him that all his chances were used up. He begged me not to leave. I said that it was too late. Then his angry tone resurfaced and he started bullying me. He lectured, "You can't leave. You have no money, no job, and nowhere to live. You'll never survive without me. If you leave again don't ever expect to come back!"

I refused to argue back and that escalated his anger. Then feeling desperate, he walked into Cammy's room and lifted her out of her crib. Holding her tight against his chest he threatened, "Fine, you can leave but the baby stays with me!"

The Keith I had known before would never have harmed her. But his behavior, now unstable and unpredictable, gave me cause for worry. Anxious, but trying to remain as calm as possible, I asked him to please hand me the baby. He refused. I asked him again and he refused again. I wasn't going to waste any more time negotiating. I lunged for the phone and dialed 911. He tried to grab it out of my hand but I held on tight. As fast as I possibly could I explained the urgency of the problem. The dispatcher said she would send an officer to the house right away.

I looked up at him and watched his demeanor change again. He stood there staring at me in disbelief as if the reality of what was happening had suddenly slapped him across the face. Then I saw a shroud of sadness overcome him. The forlorn look in his eyes said it all. He knew he had just lost every-thing.

Keith still would not let Cammy go until the sudden sound of the police officer rapping on the front door startled him. Acknowledging in his way that he knew his time had run out, he kissed Cammy on her head and then gently handed her back to me.

I ran down the steps with Cammy in my arms and answered the door. I explained everything to the officer standing there, telling him that I believed, at least for the time being, that everything was under control. But I asked him to write up a police report anyway. I wanted a record of the incident in case something happened later on.

Once everything had settled down, Keith left the house and went to work. I had to hurry up and figure out what our next move would be. I grabbed the yellow pages to look up safe houses and shelters, and then made some calls. I knew that my parents would welcome us with open arms, but after living on my own for eight years the last thing I wanted to do was run back to Mom and Dad.

There were no easy answers. I had taken an inadvisable gamble on Keith's sobriety. The time had come to face the consequences of that decision. It no longer mattered what was best for me; whatever choices I made from that moment on would have to be in the best interest of my daughter.

When Keith came home from work later that afternoon he acted as if nothing had happened. And in an effort to avoid another confrontation, I intentionally kept my distance from him. When he was downstairs I went upstairs and vice versa. He eventually came upstairs, got into bed, and went to sleep for the night. I breathed a sigh of relief. Free to roam the house as I pleased, with the baby sleeping upstairs in her crib, I tiptoed barefooted downstairs and headed for the kitchen to get a drink.

After taking two steps into the kitchen I spotted something that caused me to gasp and freeze dead in my tracks. The fractured base of a drinking glass with a four-inch jagged spike pointing straight up sat erect in the middle of the kitchen floor. Shattered glass fragments were scattered in every direction. One more step and I probably would have severed an artery. I thanked God that the baby wasn't in my arms.

Within the span of two days my life with Keith had changed from unstable to perilous. Seemingly overnight my home had become a danger zone. I had just barely avoided stepping on a land mine. Who knew what other dangers or booby traps lurked ahead? I told myself I only had to hang in there until tomorrow, just until after Keith left for work. Then I would pack up and leave forever. One more night...I could handle one more night.

Around one o'clock in the morning I awoke to the sound of the baby crying. I noticed that Keith was no longer next to me in bed. At first I thought that he might be in the baby's room. I didn't want him alone with her so I went looking for him. When I couldn't find him in the nursery I figured he'd gone downstairs. I didn't know where he was or what he was doing but I knew that he had to be up to no good. Heading down the steps to look for him I noticed that the front door was wide open. I hurried down the steps and looked outside. His car was gone.

I locked the door and laid in wait for him in the living room. He finally knocked on the door after two a.m....over an hour later. Surprised to find the door locked and me waiting there, he blurted out some bogus story about going to 7-Eleven to get cigarettes. He said he'd left the door open since he didn't have a key.

Out of everything he'd ever put me through, that act of negligence scared me the most. After what I had survived a few years before, he knew how imperative the security of the house was for me, especially while I slept. Leaving the baby and me vulnerable and defenseless that way was beyond inexcusable.

Although it was the middle of the night, I called my parents and woke them up, scaring them half to death. I explained over the phone that the baby and I were all right but Keith had relapsed again. Then I asked if I could come over and talk. They told me no problem, come right over. With that, Cammy and I were out the door.

We sat down in their living room as I recounted the unstable conditions we'd endured over the past month. It pained them to hear what Keith had put us through. Together we decided that it would be best for Cammy and me to leave Keith right away and move in with them.

I stayed with my parents until seven in the morning, the time that Keith usually left for work. Leaving Cammy safe with my parents, I went home to pack up whatever I could fit in my car. I tearfully kissed and hugged my babies Shane and Honeybell and told them I loved them. Keith loved the dogs too and I knew he'd manage to take care of them...for a little while at least. I hoped to come back and rescue them as soon as I could get on my feet.

I walked out the door. Then halfway down the path, I turned around and looked back at the house. With tears streaming down my face I said a final goodbye to my life and all my shattered dreams at Cliffedge Road.

Later that morning I called Keith's parents to ask if I could come over for a visit. They had been dangling from the same last shred of hope that I had, so I dreaded the thought of having to tell them the bad news. Understandably they took it very hard. Though acknowledging the same hopelessness as I had felt with their son, they still struggled with where to place their loyalties. I couldn't blame them; for a long time I had struggled with the same thing. They were so distraught from hearing the news that afterwards they both went to Florida indefinitely.

I slept at my parents' house that night for the first time. The next day my father suggested that we go back to the house to get Cammy's crib and anything else I didn't want destroyed. Though I never wanted to enter that house again, I agreed with my father. We had to move fast.

He drove me over there that afternoon at two thirty. I tried using my key to unlock the front door but at first it wouldn't work. It took some finagling but I finally managed to get the door open. Once inside we could see that Keith had jammed a toothpick in the lock. He had also left the dining room chair by the door, apparently for reinforcement.

First we dismantled the crib. Then we carried it outside along with the matching chest of drawers and loaded the items in the car. Next we emptied the china cabinet. Together we carefully wrapped my china, silver, and crystal wedding gifts in the newspaper and boxes that my father had wisely brought along. I took anything I thought I would need and everything of value. I only waffled on one thing; Keith's treasured baseball card collection.

Keith had saved every baseball card he'd ever gotten for the last twenty-five or more years. He had a box full of them in the basement, many which were of value. I had no entitlement to them but I also had no money. They were the only things I could have possibly liquidated for cash. Even believing that he'd somehow destroy them or sell them to buy drugs, I just didn't have the heart to take them. I pitied him. He had so very little left.

Thirty-Two: Sorting Things Out

One cannot tell when he is going to be healed, so do not try to set an exact time limit. Faith, not time will determine when the cure will be affected.
~ Paramahansa Yogananda

Cammy was only twelve weeks old when we left Cliffedge Road for the very last time. I had never intended to raise her as a single parent but sometimes life throws you curveballs. Nobody knew that better than I did.

With only the benefit of hindsight at that time in my young life, the only logical conclusion I could draw was that I would always struggle; life would always be difficult. Though I couldn't make sense of my past, I never played victim or blamed anyone. I took full responsibility for my problems and the decisions I had made that contributed to them.

It's probably hard to understand that I still loved Keith after all he'd put me through. I guess who I really loved was the person that I believed he was capable of being. Though I despised his illness and all the insanity that came with it, I never stopped loving the beautiful person I knew was hidden inside. Although rare, there were still spurts of time when that lovable person shined through.

Unfortunately those times were overshadowed by his impossible behavior.

Keith retained his family's lawyer, also a close friend of his parents, right off the bat. I hesitated to obtain legal representation because I didn't want to burden my parents with the cost of hiring an attorney, and I certainly couldn't pay for it myself. Instead I contacted the Maryland Volunteer Lawyers Service for some free advice. They sent me some literature, but basically I was on my own. Sooner or later I knew that I'd need to retain an attorney too.

I tried to be as flexible as possible when it came to Keith's visitations with Cammy. There were three stipulations that were nonnegotiable; he couldn't be high, the visits had to be on my turf, and I had to supervise all his interactions with her. Knowing he had to be cooperative in order to see his daughter, he exhibited only his best behavior.

Although he willingly gave me a hundred dollars every week for the first month of our separation, it didn't take long before my bills starting piling up. I asked for his commitment to continue our health insurance coverage, but the more I pressed him for a formal agreement the less he was willing to cooperate. Before long his compliance waned and he became more belligerent with each passing day.

On one of his visits I asked him to bring my mail to me the next time he came over; I had sent out change of address notifications but thought that some things might have crossed in the mail. He told me that I'd received nothing of importance, only junk mail. Goaded by his evasiveness, my father and I put on our detective hats and decided to launch our own investigation. I still had a key to his house so it would be easy to go over there and poke around while he was at work.

When we got there I tried to open the front door with my key but the lock wouldn't budge. Now even more determined to ferret out the truth, we walked around to the backyard pool area so I could try my key in the lock of the kitchen door. Tada! The door opened and we entered the kitchen. We didn't have to look any further; all of his opened mail, including my department store credit card bill and my bank statement, laid spread out on the dining room table. Also mixed in his mail was a bill from a lock and key service dated two days prior. *That sneaky bastard!*

My parents had rightfully lost patience with him. Keith's once relaxed visits turned into angry exchanges between my parents and him. In a fit of rage, my parents would often cross the line, critiquing Keith's interactions with Cammy. That only made things worse. I asked them not to interfere, but they had no self-control; especially when it came to their precious granddaughter. Each time he left, my parents and I would quarrel. There was no peace to be had, only drama all around me.

Keith threatened that if my parents ordered him one more time not to kiss the baby on her mouth or to be careful not to bump her head he would take her away from me. He also demanded overnight visitations with Cammy once every other weekend. There was no way; he'd have to kill me first before that would ever happen. I told him he'd have to fight me in court.

After that, I didn't want any interaction with him verbal or otherwise until I retained a lawyer. And I definitely didn't want him anywhere near Cammy. He began persistently calling my parents' house, refusing to speak to anyone but me. My parents never put his calls through; they'd tell him each time to have his lawyer contact me. In desperation he finally told my father that if he couldn't speak to me directly he would break into the house, take the baby, and go someplace where we'd never find them.

My parents graciously offered to pay my legal expenses. I hated to use their savings but I had been backed into a corner. I arranged to meet the lawyer that represented my best friend Carolyn's family and then hired him to represent me. From that day forward all communications went through our lawyers. But I still worried myself sick. I feared that a judge might ultimately grant Keith unsupervised visits or shared custody. My fears were not irrational; I'd witnessed Keith con and manipulate judges before in court. He was a pro.

Thirty-Three: The Final Rescue

Just as despair can come to one only from other human beings, hope too, can be given to one only by other human beings.
~ Elie Wiesel

I cried myself to sleep every night for the first two months of our separation. I could barely stand the emptiness I felt inside. Had it not been for Cammy I don't know how I could have pushed forward. She was the light that brightened my otherwise gloomy outlook. Through her I found the strength to keep going.

While looking in the self-help section of the library one day I stumbled upon a book by Robin Norwood entitled *Women Who Love Too Much* and recognized myself in the synopsis on the back page. I checked the book out of the library and read it cover to cover.

That book changed my life. It showed me that love was not supposed to hurt. I was finally able to stand outside of myself and see my destructive patterns and my need to fix people. I began to understand why I had made bad choices and realized that I could change my tendencies. The knowledge empowered me and I began to heal. It lit the fire of motivation under me and gave me the courage to move forward.

In order to become self-sufficient I needed to quickly learn a marketable skill. Howard Community College in Columbia, Maryland offered a one-year Optical

Assistant certificate program. I'd never get rich with that qualification but I'd definitely find a job once I graduated. My parents came through for me once again with their generous offer to fund my schooling. And my semi-retired father unselfishly volunteered to give up his part-time job in order to stay home with Cammy while I attended classes.

Meanwhile my lawyer, trying to avoid expensive litigation, attempted to negotiate an out of court settlement with Keith's lawyer. Trying his best to antagonize me, Keith agreed to give me everything that I had asked for with one provision. He wanted me to sign a legal document agreeing to allow him one unsupervised overnight visit each week with Cammy after her first birthday. He knew that I'd never agree to that; it was merely a stall tactic justifying him to ultimately refuse everything else.

Probably on the advice of his lawyer, Keith submitted himself to an outpatient methadone program in October. Methadone, a synthetic narcotic, is administered orally on a daily basis under strict conditions and guidelines. The highly monitored treatment plan kept him off the dangerous streets for awhile, but unfortunately didn't stabilize his erratic behavior.

On the morning of October twentieth, Keith called my parents' house to talk to me, but I wasn't home. I tried several times to return his call, but I was unable to get through for the entire rest of the day. He had probably taken his phone off the hook. I didn't hear from him again until four days later when he called to ask if he could see the baby. I asked him if he was "together." He said he was as together as he could be but blamed me for causing his nervous breakdown. Then he began screaming irrationally into the phone. I hung up on him as soon as the tirade started. Fortunately he didn't call back.

My mother-in-law called from Florida to speak to me two days later. I was still sleeping when the phone rang but she told my mother that an emergency situation had arisen with Keith. Her explanation had been vague; she said something about him having gone through a window but not injuring himself. She also said that she had just booked a flight to Baltimore, would be arriving later that day, and would call when she got there.

When I woke up I called her back and my father-in-law answered the telephone. He went on to explain that Keith had been spiraling downhill for the last week or so and that they truly believed Keith was losing his mind. They thought that it might be necessary to have him institutionalized. He advised that Cammy and I stay away from him in the meantime because my in-laws had no idea what he might do.

I called Keith as soon as I hung up the phone with his father. I was surprised when Keith actually picked up the phone. But his speech was unintelligible; his words intermixed with intense sorrowful crying sounded garbled. His despondency alarmed me; I feared he was suicidal. My old tendencies kicked back in and I ran to his rescue. I assured him that everything would be alright; emphasizing how much Cammy needed her Daddy. I told him to get dressed because I was coming over to take him to the doctor.

I had previously discussed Keith's addiction with a doctor friend of mine. He specialized in a holistic approach toward wellness and thought that he might be able to help. So when Keith suddenly went into crisis mode, even though it was his day off, my friend kindly agreed to see him.

Keith's moods shifted wildly as we drove to the doctor's office. My father-in-law had not exaggerated his condition; he was stark raving mad.

The pen quivered spastically between his fingers as he struggled to fill in the patient profile sheet in the waiting room. In his confusion he couldn't recall basic information; he listed me as head of the household and had to ask what my last name was.

My friend examined him and suggested a treatment plan. Of course in order to achieve results from the therapy Keith would have to thoroughly commit to the regimen. He agreed to follow through, but I knew if left to his own devices he would never persevere. I saw the situation for what it was and decided that I had done all I was willing to do. The rest was up to him.

We left the office and I hadn't even driven a block away before Keith started ripping into me. Then on sudden impulse he demanded that I stop the car. Without saying a word he opened the car door and got out, then slammed the door closed and started walking away. Glad to be rid of the insufferable thorn in my side, I left him rambling down the road and drove away.

My mother-in-law called me later in the day to let me know she had arrived. Assuming that her intended mission was to help her son, I asked if she had talked to Keith yet. I wondered if he had ever made it home. It bewildered me when she stated that she didn't intend to see him or speak to him while she was in town. She didn't even want him to know she was in Baltimore because she feared that "he might try to kill her." According to her she hadn't come to help him, only to have him committed or put in jail. None of it made sense to me, but he was her problem now. However she chose to deal or not deal with the situation was her business. I had officially washed my hands of the whole mess.

She arranged to visit Cammy the next day. Cammy had only been three months old the last time my mother-in-law had seen her. Now she was an adorable six months old and much more animated. Grandma could not get over her.

Of all the topics we covered, oddly Keith's name was never mentioned. But it was during that visit that I learned for the first time that my in-laws were putting their Baltimore condo up for sale and moving to Florida permanently. She said that they could no longer bear to stay in Baltimore and face all of its painful memories.

It's hard to convey how difficult that decision must have been for Keith's father. His entire life had revolved around the business that he had so successfully cultivated from the ground up. Over the years he had built many solid friendships with the produce wholesalers that he bought from in the wee hours of the morning. He loved his life just the way it was and hadn't had any intention of retiring or selling his business in the near future. He had really hoped to hand the business over to Keith someday, but sadly that dream would never come to fruition. Leaving Baltimore was clearly an act of exasperation; I guess he just couldn't take anymore heart-ache.

I could certainly understand his need to run away. Keith seemed to have that effect on those who loved him. I had run away from him a few times myself.

Sometimes the pain he caused became too unbearable to stand and primal urges kicked in. When fighting was no longer effective we felt impelled to flee.

Keith's mother visited with Cammy for a few hours. As she was leaving she said that if she was still in town the next day she would call me. She left the house never having mentioned Keith's name or what she planned to do about his crisis. She must have left Baltimore that same night because I never heard from her the next day.

Over the week following his mother's visit, Keith called me three or more times a day. On one of those days he also showed up at my door. I pretended that I wasn't home to avoid dealing with him. Lonely and desperate for someone to talk to, he kept calling to ask if he could see the baby. I told him each time he asked that he needed to first get better under the care of a psychiatrist because Cammy needed a well daddy. Then he'd call back the next day to tell me he was better and the pattern would start all over again. It was just like dealing with a child.

Sometimes he'd call and just make up nonsense to keep me on the phone. I tried to be patient but by the end of the week he had gotten on my last nerve. I told him to please stop calling; that I didn't have time to listen to his triviality. In retaliation he called me at six forty-five the next morning just to say that he wasn't going to give me anything I had asked for.

I was tired of him running me around in circles, tired of the games. If he wanted to act tough then I would too. I mailed a letter to his attorney stating that Keith could not visit the baby until a professional therapist advised me that he was mentally competent.

When Keith learned of the ultimatum I had imposed upon him he retaliated again, this time by cutting off my child support checks. But that wasn't the only way he exacted revenge on me. He conned his parents into believing that I was a greedy troublemaker who only wanted their money and was out to destroy all their lives. Then they lashed out at me.

After two weeks without any child support money I called Keith in desperation. I knew going into it that I might have to make a deal with the devil but I had no choice. He might have been out of his mind in many ways but not when it came to aggravating me. And just as I had expected, his game picked up right where he had left off.

When I told him that I badly needed money he said that his father had sent a check for me but he hadn't opened the envelope yet. I asked him to open the envelope and tell me the amount of the check. He refused. Then he said that he would like to start paying me one hundred fifty dollars each week, but would be deducting his medical and psychological expenses for the depression I had caused from every payment. Skipping right over his senseless bullshit I asked him when I would be receiving his father's check. He finally admitted that he had no check for me but said he'd have money for me the next day. I wasn't going to hold my breath.

On Friday evening of that same week I was casually thumbing through the Jewish Times when I was alarmed to see a realtor ad for Keith's house with a big SOLD printed over it. He had never said a word to me about selling the house, not that he was obligated to, but he was still holding my possessions hostage. I wanted my belongings out of there before it was too late. *Great! Now he had something else to hold over my head.*

I couldn't reach him that night so I called the next morning to ask if I could come over to pick up my possessions. He said I could have them if he could see Cammy that day. I said he couldn't see her so he said I couldn't have my things. Then he hung up on me. He clearly knew the terms for visitation but he was always trying to get even with me.

On November eighteenth, my attorney sent a letter to Keith's attorney asking for the return of my belongings and explaining my desperate financial circumstances. He never received a response.

In hopes that Keith would step up to the plate financially I hadn't yet considered applying for Social Service benefits. But it didn't appear that I'd ever be able to rely on Keith to give me money so I had to do something. With no prior experience I believed that the Welfare/Medicaid system had been set up to help people in my situation. What I didn't realize was that you had to know how to "work" the system in order to qualify for benefits.

I set up an appointment with a caseworker, brought all the required documents and went through the application process. At the time the only asset I had in my name was my Grand Prix. I never even considered transferring ownership of the car out of my name, but I should have. The system denied my eligibility for benefits because the value of my car was higher than the allowable assets. WIC was the only government assistance that I could get. Once I knew, I transferred the title of my car out of my name and into my father's. Then I began the appeal process. After several weeks of waiting I was denied again.

After working on my separation and custody case for three months my lawyer had gotten nowhere. He had tried his best for an out of court settlement, hoping to save my parents some money. But Keith had used my passivity to his benefit. He'd continue to play his vindictive games as long as he could get away with it. I felt it best to terminate my attorney's legal services and hire someone else to represent me.

The fight was about to get very expensive. That might have been fine if I stood to gain anything financially, but I didn't. My parents were not wealthy people, but they would have spent any amount of money to protect Cammy and assure my custody of her. All I needed from Keith was child-support and healthcare. I wasn't asking for much. Oh yeah...and he had to be sound of mind and sober if he ever wanted to see his daughter!

Thirty-Four: Sweet Revenge

*Fall seven times, stand up
eight.*
~ *Japanese Proverb*

Encouraging me to start dating, my married girlfriends began introducing me to their single guy friends. After all I'd been through with Keith the thought of dating sickened me. One would imagine I'd find the prospect of dating potentially "normal" guys refreshing. But truthfully, after living with drama for so many years, I worried that they would all bore me to tears. And besides, what young, single guy would want to date a woman who was still nursing her baby? How awkward!

But honestly, leaving all insecurities aside, I really did welcome the attention. It helped to fill up the emptiness for a little while.

With the determination to get my post-pregnant body back into dating shape I joined a health club. I went there with Carolyn, also a member, and circuit trained three nights a week. I proudly wore a bikini in no time flat.

The optical program at school had captivated my interest; I looked forward to attending my classes each day. My grades reflected my enthusiasm; I made the Dean's list both semesters. I also made some very nice friends. But best of all, going to school every day redirected the focus of my largely dysfunctional life.

Cammy was thriving in the care of my parents. My father would play with her for hours every afternoon. He'd use flash cards to teach her a variety of things and then demonstrate what she had learned when I came home from school each day. I used to tell him that she was his "trained monkey" because he always had her performing! I think it was the happiest time in his life.

My mother took great pleasure in cooking special foods for her and watching her eat. To a Jewish mother food equals love. Cammy was the light of their lives. I didn't know how I could ever thank my parents for all they were doing for us.

With that said, and as grateful as I was for my parents' help, it wasn't an ideal living arrangement for me. New mother that I was, I sometimes resented having to parent under the watchful eyes of Cammy's impassioned, overprotective grandparents. I'm not trying to deprecate their actions in any way; they were amazing grandparents with only the best interest of their granddaughter in mind. But I had no personal space to call my own and no boundaries with my parents. My father would walk into my room, even with the door closed, any time of the day or night to tell me what to I should do with my baby. In sheer frustration I'd fly off the handle, using expletives that I never thought I'd say to *anyone*, let alone my father.

I had come full circle. I was the child again, miserably living in my childhood home, desperate for serenity and harmony. And I felt guilty for feeling the way I did; my parents were sacrificing everything to help me and my baby. It was all very confusing. I had no idea who I was. My happiness wasn't coming from inside of me; it was entirely dependent on the actions and the moods of the people around me.

I needed my own place but my hands were tied; that wouldn't happen until I finished school in a year and found a job.

With my love for Cammy at the core of my being and my steadfast determination to give her a happy life, I remained focused on our future. She was the absolute source of my strength.

That December, my new attorney jumped right on the case and issued a five-page *Complaint for custody and limited divorce* to the circuit court for Baltimore County. Among other requests, she asked for the court to sign an Injunction preventing Keith from transferring, disposing of, or selling any of my personal property. And in her cover letter to Keith's attorney she wrote, *I am sure that your client does not need any more legal entanglements at the present time and would ask that you kindly convey to him the importance of returning these items to my client immediately.* The letter was drafted on December fourth; the settlement on Keith's house was scheduled for December thirtieth.

Upon receipt of the letter, Keith's lawyer advised him to arrange a time with me when I could enter the house and claim my belongings. I don't know why he was making such a big deal out of it; I only wanted the property that I had acquired before marriage. As far as I was concerned, the court could decide the rest.

Prompted by his attorney, Keith named a specific morning that week that he'd leave the front door unlocked so I could retrieve my property. Since a small amount of bulky furniture was involved I scheduled a mover to help me.

On the arranged morning I met the mover in front of the Cliffedge Road house. He walked up to the front door with me ready to get started. But when I tried to open the door I couldn't; it was locked. We both walked around to the back door and I tried that doorknob but it was also locked. The young mover looked at me and said, "Do you want me to go in through the window? I do it all the time."

It was finally my turn for retribution. Keith thought he was so smart but I was about to beat him at his own game. "Do it!" I pronounced.

The guy walked around to the side of the house and jimmied the living room window open. Then he climbed in, unlocked the front door, and let me in.

"What am I taking?" he asked me.

"That bastard is going to pay for this. I'm taking everything!" I exclaimed.

Under my direction the mover carried out my belongings and all of our new furniture. I took anything and everything of value including the sheets, blanket and comforter right off our bed. I even took the alarm clock we'd shared. I figured if I didn't take what I wanted right then and there, I'd probably never see any of it again. He'd inevitably sell or destroy everything.

As we pulled off our caper, the adrenaline surging in my body caused by an amalgam of excitement, fear, and vengefulness, made me feel manic. I'd never done anything like that before. The biggest problem with the unexpectedly large booty I was about to make off with was where to put it all. My parents' house was small and already busting at the seams. But at the time I was way too pumped up to worry about those trivial details.

My father came outside when he saw my car pull up with the moving van behind me. While I was gone he'd rearranged some things to make space for the furniture he had expected me to bring home. I met him in the carport wearing a sheepish look on my face. The mover got out of his truck and said, "Where do you want everything?"

I turned away from my father and towards the guy, then discreetly raised my index finger while mouthing the words "Wait a minute." He nodded back at me in acknowledgement. I looked back at my father and said, "Dad, I've done something crazy." Then I explained the whole course of events.

My father looked noticeably perturbed. His immediate concerns were both obvious and legitimate; where would we put everything and what would Keith do when he found out?

We decided not to make the mover wait any longer and instructed him to unload everything into the open carport. We'd work on a solution after he left. The driver emptied out the truck then pulled away leaving us both standing dumbfounded in front of the jam-packed carport. Now coming down from my "high," I began to worry about the repercussions of my rash act.

Not even an hour had passed before Keith called. He'd already come home, found the furniture missing, and was going ape-shit! I had to hold the phone away from my ear to avoid the deafening impact of his bellowing threats. He demanded that his furniture be returned immediately, claiming that he'd have me arrested for breaking, entering, and theft if I didn't comply. He obstinately declared that he was coming right over and then hung up on me.

Even though I had no way to hide the evidence, I didn't believe Keith would call the police. With his parole violations and outstanding warrants they would have immediately arrested him. And if by chance I had to defend myself, I'd explain that I was permitted access to the house and had legal entitlement to my property. They would have believed my story over his any day. Still the whole thing made me nervous. I didn't want to deal with his wrath.

In actuality Keith knew he was powerless over me. The only weapon he had was his big mouth.

Within the half-hour Keith came strolling on foot down the street toward my parents' house. His driver's license had been revoked; heaven knows what had happened to his car. My father and I stood guard in the carport amidst the evidence. Keith swaggered up the driveway, dressed well with his head held high, affecting an air of dignity. He looked gaunt and emaciated. Although he was all puffed up, trying to appear big and important, the wind could have blown him over. Calmer than I expected and very polite, he spoke authoritatively, intending to intimidate me.

He fired off his usual threats even though he knew they'd fall on deaf ears. He tried bargaining with me but got nowhere. I told him to leave or I'd call the police. He backed down but with one last threat--I'd be hearing from his lawyer. With that said he walked back up the street, heading home I suppose.

I don't know what transpired but he never sold the house on Cliffedge Road. Ultimately he reported the robbery without implicating me, filed a claim with his homeowner's insurance company, and ended up receiving a sizable cash settlement. In the end he made out better than I did. *Go figure!*

Thirty-Five: Summer at the Falls

A person often meets his destiny on the road he took to avoid it.
~ Jean de la Fontaine

Keith didn't want to go to court because that meant losing the hold he had over me. He knew that once he lost that control he'd lose me forever; he thought he'd lose Cammy too. The hate he directed at me was actually rooted in love. That was the only way he knew to get my attention, to keep me in his life. As it is said, negative attention is better than no attention at all. The poor guy was so sick, so desperate.

On January 6, 1986 in response to the complaint filed by my attorney, The Circuit Court issued a writ of summons to be served in person to Keith within sixty days. Once the server placed the document in his hand, Keith had thirty days to sign and return it or he'd lose the case by default.

The Sheriff's office made several unsuccessful attempts to serve Keith. After all his run-ins with the law he knew how to spot and dodge the servers. The only way to get the writ into his hand was to catch him off guard. I hired a private investigator that specialized in just that thing. I scheduled a time on January tenth for Keith to come over to see Cammy. Knowing that he'd be walking over, the detective waited on the sidewalk up the street, posed as a neighbor. As Keith approached him the private detective created a distraction and put the summons right in his hand. He was successfully served!

Having to display his best behavior if he wanted to see his daughter, Keith managed to pull himself together one day each week. My father-in-law provided the child-support money that Keith brought over with him when he came to visit Cammy. I had never intended to deprive him of a relationship with Cammy. All I asked from him was a reasonable amount of normalcy.

Every time he visited he brought her a thoughtful gift. At home with little else to do, he would videotape hours and hours of cartoons for Cammy to watch. When he came over to visit, he'd give the tape to me as a gift for her, then go home and make another one for his next visit. After such a loving gesture, I didn't have the heart to tell him that she had no interest in cartoons and would never watch any of them.

Cammy turned one year old on Tuesday, May 6, 1986. I had her birthday party on the prior weekend at my parents' house with family and friends. Keith didn't come; he was too emotional and most likely too high to face all those people.

Her birthday fell right on Passover that year. My mother kept a kosher home so she had to improvise with the party menu. She baked a delicious *pesachdik* sponge cake, one of her specialties, and I put a big "1" candle on top. Everything else was served with *matzoh*. My mother's food was so yummy; no one even noticed the substitutions.

Cam had been a small baby from birth. At a year old she weighed no more than sixteen pounds. She wasn't lanky though; her arms had creases all the way up that my mother referred to as "bracelets." And after being born practically bald she had grown silky fine, golden blond hair. She was such a little cutie-pie; everyone wanted to hold her. But Cammy was only comfortable when women held her. She cried if a man besides her Granddad picked her up. Like mother, like daughter! Ironic isn't it?

As of her first birthday she hadn't begun to walk, though she did let go and stand up by herself for the first time at her party. She didn't start walking until she was fifteen months old. I didn't mind carrying her around since she was still small...and very cuddly.

On the Tuesday of her actual birthday Keith came over to see her. He looked good; he was well dressed as usual but very thin. He walked into the house carrying a great big box; I don't know how he actually carted it over to the house on foot. He sat the box down on the floor and handed me an envelope. He told me it was a birthday card for Cammy and asked me to please save it and show it to her when she was old enough to understand. He wanted her to always know how very much he loved her.

Anxious to give Cammy her gift, Keith wasted no time in opening the big cardboard box. He reached in and pulled out a child-sized, molded-plastic fruit-stand; complete with a cash register, assorted plastic fruit, and little price stakes that fit into holes in each bin. Coming from him the gift could not have been more perfect. I pictured Cammy looking just like her Daddy as she sold her fruit to make-believe customers.

He was watching my face. I could see how happy it made him to know that I liked the present. On such a joyous day, just the first of so many happy future occasions, it made me sad to think of all he would miss out on. He loved us both with all his heart; we meant everything to him. Tragically that love could not save him.

My child custody case went before a Master on May 22, 1986. Our legally established separation date was July 26, 1985. My attorney represented me that afternoon; Keith waived his right to counsel. After hearing both sides the court awarded full custody of Cammy to me. That lifted a huge weight off my mind.

Keith was awarded two supervised visitations per week, one hour each, at my home. The conditions of visitation were that he could not use drugs unless prescribed by a physician and that he had to furnish my attorney with weekly urinalysis. The Master, sympathizing with Keith's circumstances, ordered him to pay only fifty dollars per week for child support. I thought that was grossly unfair. We were both ordered to undergo psychiatric evaluations by the medical office of the Baltimore County Circuit Court.

On Memorial Day, five days after the hearing, I graduated from Howard Community College, Summa Cum Laude with a Certificate of Proficiency in Vision Care. My life was finally moving forward; the future looked much brighter.

I'd become more comfortable with dating and had an active social life. With Cammy weaned, breastfeeding was no longer a hang-up for me. Wherever I went Cammy went (with a few exceptions); we were a packaged deal. After some dating experience I discovered that "normal" guys could be lots of fun.

My focus had changed; I hoped to find a nice guy that loved us both to build a new family with. I wanted her to have a stable daddy to love her and be there for her. I knew it would take a phenomenal man to rise to that challenge. I wondered if he even existed.

Even though my life was gradually moving forward, I was despondent. Things weren't changing fast enough and that frustrated me. I wanted my own home, still had no income, and was profoundly lonely. My self-esteem was at an all-time low. I didn't believe that any decent guy would ever want me or that I had anything worthwhile to offer. I had made a mess of my life and I couldn't see how things would ever get better. I was stuck in a rut.

My girlfriend Debbie, who had originally given Keith my telephone number, had separated from her husband shortly after I had. Her situation was the exact opposite of mine. Her soon-to-be ex-husband had purchased a townhouse for her and was keeping her comfortable with alimony and child support payments. He was an involved father who stayed close with their one-year old son.

Debbie invited me to join her on a singles cruise that summer. I would have loved to go along with her but I had no money.

As her luck would have it she took the cruise alone and met a nice guy from California. After the cruise ended and they had gone home to their respective coasts he invited her to visit him in California. She planned to spend two weeks with him there. And since her house would be empty, she offered it to me and Cammy. I jumped at the chance; I desperately needed some privacy.

She lived in a very nice development called The Falls. The homeowners' amenity that I most looked forward to taking advantage of was the community pool. My summer vacation would be fourteen glorious days relaxing by the pool with my daughter.

I bought Cammy an inflatable safety ring especially designed for babies so she could float around in the pool with me. One afternoon we were swimming in the pool along with an older woman who kept smiling at us. At one point she swam closer, and then with a broken Russian accent commented, "*Shiksa* mommy, *Shiksa* baby!" I don't know what possessed her to say that but I think she meant it as a compliment. I remembered people making that comment about me as a child and now I had a daughter that looked like a *Shiksa* too!

During weekdays very few residents came to the pool. I was pleasantly surprised to see lots of young singles from the community when the weekend rolled around. On the first Saturday we were there, while relaxing on a lounge chair with Cammy playing on a blanket beside me, I watched two guys enter the pool area. One was taller than the other; the shorter guy had dark hair and a very dark tan. I thought he looked Mexican. They hung around for awhile but we never spoke.

Later that day I was craving a snowball so Cammy and I drove into town. The snowball is a Maryland summer delicacy right up there with steamed crabs. It's basically shaved ice only it's served in a regular cup rather than a cone-shaped cup.

I parked my car on Reisterstown Road, right in front of the snowball stand that stood next to Field's Pharmacy. When I got out of my car I noticed the shorter dark skinned guy that I'd seen earlier that day at the pool talking to the two guys working there. After seeing him up close I determined that he wasn't Mexican, just very tan. I approached him and mentioned that I'd seen him earlier in the day at The Falls pool. He said he remembered me and added, "You're the babysitter that was sitting there next to the blond-haired baby on the blanket." The details of his observation were amazing considering I never saw him look my way!

"I'm not the babysitter, I'm her mother," I remarked, laughingly. I introduced myself then pointed to the car seat in the back of my car. "That's my daughter Cammy."

He said his name was Billy and then he introduced me to his younger brother and his brother's friend, the co-owners of the snowball stand. Billy seemed like a nice guy. He asked me if my daughter and I would be coming to the pool the next day and invited us to hang out there with him and his friends. After I got my snowball I thanked him and said we'd definitely see him tomorrow.

When Cammy and I came to the pool the next day, Billy greeted us warmly and introduced us to his friends. We spent the entire afternoon at the pool with them and then were invited to join them later at one of their houses. I had more fun that day than I'd had in years.

Billy and I became good friends. He was twenty-three years old, four and a half years younger than I was. As young as he was, he really had his act together and he already owned his own home. There was definitely chemistry between us and we went out a few times, but he was much too young to take seriously. He did adore Cammy though, and she liked him too.

After meeting Billy, I met and dated a handful of other single guys, ranging in age from twenty-three to fifty-something, living in the complex. I'd never had such a good time; I didn't want to leave! But after two weeks, my girlfriend came home and I had to go back to my parents' house. That was a tremendous letdown. But even then I continued my friendship with Billy and still dated a few of the guys.

My oldest suitor had taken a vested interest in me. He was a successful real estate agent, divorced with grown kids, and fairly well connected. After learning of my financial hardships and accumulating legal fees, he asked his attorney friend to represent me Pro Bono. Believe me, there was no greater gift that anyone could have given me at that time. I humbly accepted his offer.

Things seem to happen when you least expect them to. There are no coincidences and no random occurrences. Those pivotal two weeks at The Falls would change the course of my life forever.

Thirty-Six: Baby Steps

Hope is a higher heart frequency,
and as you begin to re-connect
with your heart, hope is waiting
to show new possibilities and ar-
rest the downward spiral of grief
and loneliness.
~ *Sara Paddison*

With the legalities of our separation behind us, Keith no longer had reason to create friction between his parents and me. Though long distance, the close relationship we'd always shared continued. They missed Cammy terribly; she was the only bright spot in their life. No matter what happened in the future we'd always have her to bind us together.

At the end of July, Cammy and I flew to Boca to vacation with my in-laws. Their apartment offered exciting new territory for Cammy to explore. Even though she wasn't walking yet, she managed to get around pretty well, cruising from one piece of furniture to the other. Her favorite new discovery was Grandma's makeup table. It was low enough for her to reach and she could play with all the different shaped containers. She also loved Grandma's closet with all her sparkly shoes.

Every morning the three of us rode to the beach club in the Rolls Royce convertible with the top down. Grandpa slept during those hours so he

217

didn't join us. We'd stay on the beach until naptime and then I'd lay her down to sleep on a palm tree shaded lounge chair by the pool with her favorite little pillow.

Cammy had never stepped on sand before. The first time I tried to put her down she drew her knees up and adamantly refused to put her feet down. Each day we had to create a blanket camp between our lounge chairs so her feet never had to touch the sand.

After a nice day at the beach club, the four of us would dress up and go out to eat. Grandma ordered Cammy all her favorite foods at the restaurants, including lobster.

My in-laws wanted me to find a boyfriend in Florida with the hope that we'd ultimately move closer to them. My mother-in-law tried her best to nudge things along. While we were out to dinner each evening she would brazenly approach nice looking guys, ask them if they were single, and then introduce me to them. Typically the guy would ask if I was her daughter. She'd tell him no, I was her daughter-in-law. Then she'd say, "That's okay, she's divorcing my son!" The guys were left speechless. It was hilarious.

We had a wonderful time in Boca. I was thankful that our relationship had survived even though my marriage to their son hadn't. Their enduring relationship with Cammy meant even more to me.

After the completion of two relaxing summer vacations, playtime was over. It was time for me to focus my attention on finding a job. I'd hardly begun to look when the perfect job fell right into my lap.

After running into a high school friend who I hadn't seen in ten years, I happened to mention that I was looking for a job in the eye-care industry. She said that her fiancé was an Optometrist who was going to be managing a brand new Pearle Vision Eye Lab. They hadn't hired their staff yet, but she knew that he would need an office manager and suggested that I call him. He in turn recommended me to the owner who interviewed me and then offered me the job. The store was scheduled to open in October.

In the mean time my new attorney sent Keith notification of the Complaint for Absolute Divorce that he had filed with the Court. Keith had eighteen days to answer the complaint. After receiving no response, my attorney filed a request for an Order of Default, and a Master's hearing was scheduled for February 11, 1987. I was more than anxious to finalize the divorce; we had been separated since July 1985.

My youthful sixty-three-year-old father had not worked outside the home in over a year. He never complained, but I knew he needed more stimulation. Though I didn't like the idea of putting Cammy in day-care I was willing to consider it under the right circumstances. I turned to my favorite classified publication, The Jewish Times.

A woman offering day-care in her home drew me to a listing so I called for more information. She had one child, a daughter who was the same age as Cammy, and she was looking for one child to care for. Though it was only a preliminary screening, I liked what I heard. She sounded like a warm, loving person and very safety-conscious. We arranged to meet at her house.

I felt even more comfortable when I met her face to face. She was wonderful with Cammy and the two little girls became fast friends. After spending a few hours chatting and observing I knew Cammy would be happy, safe, and well provided for there. I made the decision to entrust her with my precious daughter.

Eyelab opened and I started working there in October. I'd drop Cammy off at daycare every morning at 9:00 a.m. Monday through Friday and pick her up every evening at six. I took great pride in having taken my first steps towards independence. And most importantly both of us were happy.

Thirty-Seven: Thwarted

Living involves tearing up one rough draft after another.

~ Author Unknown

Before long the winter holidays were upon us. Keith came over to visit Cammy carrying a shopping bag full of Hanukah gifts he had chosen for her. His choices were random, nothing of value but nevertheless thoughtful. Some items still had price tags hanging on them. Nothing was wrapped.

Keith continued his visitations, though I only allowed him to see Cammy when he was sober. He had significantly calmed down; outside of his once-a-week visits I had very few dealings with him. I was anxiously counting the days until I could finalize my divorce in February. I hoped for a simple hearing before the Master; I didn't even expect Keith to appear or give testimony.

Unpredictably, on the day of the hearing Keith walked into the Master's Chambers at the scheduled time. I was already waiting there with my attorney, my father, and Carolyn as my witness. Keith had come alone.

The Master took my testimony first. I had filed for divorce on the grounds of voluntary separation. Among other things, I stated that Keith had agreed to the separation and that there was no hope of re-

221

conciliation. Carolyn backed up my testimony with firsthand knowledge.

When it was Keith's turn to testify he denied ever agreeing to the separation. He said that he'd asked me to remain with him a number of times. In addition he explained to the Master that he had no money, no job, and that his father was paying his fifty-dollar per week child support. He admitted to giving daily urinalysis at the drug center but complained that I was still refusing his visitation rights.

After hearing Keith's sob story, the Master was sympathetic and sided with him. The Master stated in his final report, *"There is a serious question in my mind as to whether or not the defendant can make child support payments as previously ordered, in view of the fact that he hasn't been employed."* And he denied my divorce due to *"reasonable doubt that grounds of voluntary separation existed at the time of separation."*

Keith had screwed me again.

Just one week after our hearing took place Keith was locked up on charges of theft. His sentence for the crime was one and a half months in the county jail. During Keith's incarceration, his brother Mike, who may or may not have been residing in the Clif-fedge Road house, set it on fire. The damage was estimated at over fifty-one thousand dollars, the house uninhabitable.

I was thankful to have retrieved everything of value, though I kicked myself for not having taken his valuable baseball card collection. All that remained of his lifetime collection were ashes.

After the disappointment of having my divorce denied, there was still a bright spot for me that February; Cammy and I moved out of my parents' house and into our own apartment.

Our affordable two-bedroom apartment spanned the entire first floor of a small row-home that was situated in a quiet, older neighborhood. The first floor of our apartment led outside to a small fenced in back yard, and even included a semi-finished basement, complete with a washer and a dryer. It was by no means perfect but it was mine. I'd finally achieved the independence I'd worked so hard for.

I had barely raised my head above the surface of the water, when out of nowhere a gigantic tidal wave came and knocked me under again. All the personal data that I'd voluntarily submitted to my new employer and landlord had appeared on my credit report. Any creditor that had my social security number also had access to my new home address. With excellent credit and nothing to hide I hadn't given it a second thought. I'd been unaware that Hurricane Keith had hit land and was barreling in my direction.

Meanwhile the credit departments of two major department stores and two major credit-card companies had been delighted to find out my new address. They'd apparently gotten nowhere mailing my statements to Keith's house. There was only one problem...I hadn't purchased anything on those accounts. Past due itemized statements in my name amounting to several thousand dollars started coming in the mail. I was mortified! I'd never applied for credit with the two credit-card companies who were now billing me. A few years before I'd applied for credit to buy an appliance at one of the stores and never purchased anything else. The other department store account had been inactive for the last couple of years.

It was an inconceivable mess. As a single parent of a toddler and working a full-time job, I already had more than my share to handle. Though I believed that my allegations of fraud would eventually absolve me of all responsibility, I still worried myself sick. I had no idea how long and how hard I'd have to fight the battle to clear my name. I was appalled at what I discovered when I began to retrace Keith's steps.

I found out that after I'd moved out of Keith's house, one credit-card company had sent an unsolicited application to me at that address. The only requirements to open the account were a check mark and a signature. Keith (and/or his brother) checked the box, signed my name, and mailed it back. Then the company sent my credit card to Cliffedge Road. Prompted by my complaint an investigation was launched. They determined that the signature on the application was fraudulent, apologized to me, and immediately closed the account. I was not held responsible for any of the charges.

As if he hadn't done enough damage, Keith (and/or his brother) had picked up an application at a gas station, filled in my personal information, and submitted it. That company approved the application then mailed my credit card to the Cliffedge Road address. After several months and a slew of phone calls and certified letters, the charges were eventually deemed fraudulent. But a small portion of the balance that they claimed I owed but I refused to pay remained due. Consequently a blemish remained on my personal credit history for the next ten years.

From what I could gather Keith must have scoured our local mall looking for stores where I had active credit accounts.

I'd opened a credit account at one department store in that mall, solely in my name, before I'd even met him. Keith never knew it existed. I don't know how he pulled it off, but he went to the store in person and conned the credit department into allowing him to make purchases on my account for only that day. Then he had them change the address to his so I wouldn't find out what he had done. Believe me when I tell you that he did a lot of damage in that one day. I pleaded my case and won. But that deceit felt the most personal; many of Cammy's Hanukah gifts, still with hanging price tags, were listed on the sale itemization of that statement. I returned whatever I could.

When Keith tried the other store where we had originally purchased the appliance, he hit the lottery. He never had his own credit so I had opened the account in my name and listed him as an authorized user. I never gave him a card to use or used the account myself after that. After we had separated, I cancelled all of our joint accounts but forgot that he had been approved as a user of that card. Once the damage was done it didn't matter how hard I fought the charges, I was completely liable for the debt. I couldn't afford to pay off the bill so the department store issued a judgment against me. That resulted in ten years of irreparable damage to my credit score.

Not only had that S.O.B. left me penniless, he'd also destroyed the only thing I had left to fall back on.

Thirty-Eight: The Letter

It does not matter how deep you fall, what matters is how high you bounce back.
~ Author Unknown

Cammy turned two years old on May 6, 1987. I hadn't heard from Keith in weeks and he didn't come to visit her on her birthday. On May 7th he wrote and mailed the following letter to me:

Dear Randi,

I hope this letter is read before it reaches the trashcan. It's the most sincere hurt I've faced (writing this) straight in years.

I can only start with "if only I had done" but that hardly does much after the way I've disrupted your life, past and future. I would never bother with the puny words "I'm sorry" as that would be like putting a Band-Aid on a broken leg.

As I'm sure you know I'm in Sinai (hospital) with pneumonia. Also, I'm aware everyone realizes my circumstances over the last what seems forever. So, I got my pneumonia from the weakness of my body resistance as I was withdrawing from the pills and methadone. I finally decided after three tries (all with seizures) at coming off Valium that I'd try to do it in the hospital. That was two weeks ago, with no signs of getting out. I'm definitely paying the price for my sins.

Randi, it took about a week before I could even begin to scratch the surface of what I did to you. Amazingly, the one particular night that most stands out with the most pain is the night in New York City when you couldn't bring yourself to make love with me. I knew you weren't playing or punishing me, as your honesty wouldn't permit such a game to be played. Later we went to Sardi's Restaurant and I talked the truth. I knew when you couldn't do it with me earlier that our life together would be over unless I did the most drastic event. Tell the truth! And I did! It hurt you so bad. If ever I wanted my life to end, it was then. I still was so much in love with you but I could not stop the drugs. I had to sit and watch that pain in your face. For the last week I've seen that beautiful face every time I can't somehow relax for a little time.

There are so many more times I haven't begun to suffer like I know God is going to make me suffer. If only I could have cried all day in the rehab like I do here, I possibly could have stuck it out drug-free. If only.

I never admitted that it was you I love and miss and need as much as Cammy. I only had to admit that of my child. I can't hide from myself anymore as the doctors have told me my body will not withstand anymore withdrawals. I'll die from taking the drug or I'd die trying to come off. I know they aren't just scaring me because three different sections of doctors, unrelated, told the same story. My body is equal to that of a 65 year-old man (and I feel like it). Even my mind finally went. Remember how I could count? Give me numbers on paper now and my answer will probably be wrong. If you ask me what I did yesterday you'll get a blank stare.

In closing, I have of course no illusions of you and I. However, I do have illusions of being a father to my child. Only you can decide if my illusions are just that... illusions. Please consider my desire without thought of revenge. I may not have years to watch <u>our</u> child grow up as my health is so wacked. I would not see her if sickness could in any way spread.

I wish you the happiest of Mother's Day and wish you were not another single mother. I'm certain you are the finest mother in the universe! I wish I was able to be out to get you something, but...I'll make it up.

I <u>still</u> love you,
Keith

I knew that the real Keith, the person I could never stop loving, had written that letter. With tears in my eyes I read his tragic thoughts again and again. He had said all the words that I'd longed to hear. I only needed one more thing to complete the closure. I had to go see him. Knowing how emotional that visit would be I asked Carolyn to come with me for support.

When I entered his hospital room his face beamed exactly like it did the very first time I ever saw him. He thanked me over and over for coming. He was sicker than I'd ever seen him but more lucid than he had been in years. The real Keith, the adorable man that I had fallen in love with, was lying in the hospital bed before me. He spoke honestly.

I looked at him, wondering for the umpteenth time what torment lie buried deep in his soul. How could someone as lovable as he was feel so unworthy of being loved? What drove him to self-mutilate and self-destruct? I'd never know the real reasons; they lay hidden fathoms beneath his tragic flaw. Sometimes there are no answers; for the sake of my sanity I'd been forced to come to terms with that.

When I left the hospital I didn't know if I'd ever see him again, but I finally had closure.

He eventually recovered from the pneumonia and went home. But his body was a ticking time bomb. It couldn't take much more abuse.

Thirty-Nine: The Shining White Knight

There are two kinds of sparks. One goes off with a hitch like a match, but it burns quickly. The other is the kind that needs time, but when the flame strikes...it's eternal.
~ Timothy Oliveira

I had reentered the dating scene concerned that having a child would scare men off. But with a few exceptions the opposite turned out to be true. Sometimes I wondered who the guy liked more, me or Cammy.

I had found no shortage of men to date. The Optometrist I worked with pretty much summed up my situation in a poem he had written about me and read at one of our company parties. I'll never forget that humorous line--*With dates for lunch and dates for dinner, does anyone wonder how she keeps getting thinner?*

The guys that I had met were all very nice but not exactly what I was looking for. I'd often *kvetch* to Carolyn that I'd never find "the one." She kept telling me to be patient. One day while we were having one of those recurring discussion she said to me, "You know you ought to take another look at your friend Billy. He's very handsome, adores Cammy, and has everything you've been looking for."

It was like she flipped a switch and the light inside my head turned on. Everything she said was true. Because of his age I had never considered him as husband or father material. But the more I thought about her suggestion the more sense it made to me. He was the perfect guy for me in every way and exactly the kind of male role model I wanted for Cammy.

Billy called on Memorial Day asking me if I wanted to get together. I told him that I had a tentative date but the guy hadn't called yet. He said, "Blow him off and come out with me." So that's exactly what I decided to do. I knew I'd have more fun with him anyway.

Billy picked me up at my house late in the afternoon and we headed over to the Mt. Washington Tavern to meet his friends. As we walked from his car to the restaurant I reached over and touched his hand. When he took my hand in his an intimacy we had never before shared flowed between us. No words were necessary; we both knew it was right. From that day forward Billy, Cammy, and I were inseparable.

Billy is the oldest of three siblings. I had already met his younger brother at the snowball stand the same day that I'd first met Billy, but I hadn't met his sister yet. I knew that the three of them were very close.

His sister loved horses and took riding lessons at a nearby ranch. One afternoon Billy brought Cammy and me with him to watch her ride. His parents had also come to watch her ride that day so I had the opportunity to meet all three of them. I don't think he'd told his parents anything about us yet; it probably shocked them to see their twenty-four year old son with a young mother and child. His friendly sister greeted us warmly; his parents were cordial.

Billy and his father worked together in their family owned Food Broker business. And when Billy came to work the next morning his father took him to task. He wanted to know what Billy was doing with that *Shiksa* and her child. Billy just laughed and said, "She's not a *Shiksa*, she's more Jewish than we are!"

After we got that out of the way Cammy and I became very close with his family. Billy's parents loved and treated Cammy as if she were their own granddaughter. His sister and brother became instant aunt and uncle to her.

Our families had very similar values and traditions. We discovered that before Billy even existed, his grandmother and uncle both knew me as a little girl. Prior to my *Bubbe* and *Zaide's* move to their house near The Plaza, they had lived in the same neighborhood where Billy's grandparents owned a store. I spent a lot of time at my grandparents' house, and my uncle who lived with them used to walk me to that store all the time. It turned out that our families knew each other well.

Billy couldn't have possibly loved Cammy more if she were his flesh and blood. In Cammy's adoring eyes, he was her Daddy. She called him Billy but it sounded more like "Beewee." There was nothing he wouldn't do for her. He changed diapers, fed her, and bathed her. If she got tired while we were out he'd carry her across his arms while she slept. He even sat next to her on the floor of the bathroom while she learned to use the potty, reading book after book to her until she'd do something. I would not have had the patience to sit with her as long as he did!

With Cammy's best interest in mind, Keith faded into the background. He knew that Billy had stepped up to the plate, and he didn't want to interfere. I never asked him to stay away; he made that decision entirely on his own. He loved Cammy too much to subject her to the insanity of his life. Through his selfless act he gave his beloved daughter the greatest gift of all--the happy life she deserved.

Keith's parents remained a constant in our lives; we spoke often. Cammy and I went to Florida and had another wonderful visit with them. I encouraged their involvement in Cammy's life; they were the link to the father she'd probably never get to know.

If it hadn't been for Keith's father I would have never received any child support. He had taken that responsibility on from the beginning. He also paid the tuition for three years of pre-school. I could not have afforded to send her to such a fine school on my own. I knew I could always count on his help if I ever needed it. There was nothing he wouldn't have done for his granddaughter.

I enrolled Cammy in pre-school when she was two and a half years old. Though still very young, she thrived on intellectual stimulation. She could never soak up enough knowledge. When she wasn't being taught she'd play teacher to an invisible class. That was her way of learning new things. That was also the year she met her imaginary friends, Winnie and Bobbitz. They seemed so real; I suspected that they were her guardian angels. I couldn't see them but she could. She'd carry on long conversations with them while they played together. I'd even watched her push them on the swings. They stayed with her until she started elementary school.

Between ages two and three Cammy developed her signature look, golden-blonde curly hair. She attracted an annoying amount of attention from strangers that thought nothing of touching her head. It mostly bothered me when weirdoes touched her; I wanted to smack their hands away. Billy had curly hair too but his was dark. People often told him how much his "daughter" looked like him. He liked hearing that. I actually don't know from whom she inherited the curls but it certainly wasn't from me. The longer her hair grew, the springier it became. I referred to the bounciest curls as "boing" curls.

Ironically Cammy had been born bald. But I remember my mother telling me that bald babies end up with the most beautiful hair. I thought she was making that up but it turned out that she was right. Good call Mom!

Forty: Under the Chuppa

A good marriage is one which allows for change and growth in the individuals and in the way they express their love.
~ Pearl S. Buck

I received notice in August that my second divorce hearing had been scheduled. After two years and one month of sheer lunacy the whole *focacta* mess was about to end.

Keith's whereabouts were unknown. He hadn't resided on Cliffedge Road since the fire in March, but he had arranged for the forwarding of his mail to an undisclosed location. The court had mailed him notification of the hearing but he never responded.

I appeared before a different master of the court on September 10, 1987. Keith, still M.I.A., never showed up at the hearing. My revised allegation, two-year separation, was indisputable. I brought Carolyn along to corroborate that fact. After the longest twenty-six months of my life, the court finally granted my divorce. I was free, free, free at last! Hallelujah, praise the Lord!

Four blissful, Keithless months passed by before receiving the following correspondence from his attorney:

Dear Randi

I received a letter from Keith who is in the Baltimore County Detention Center and he expects to be out around the first of February. He would like to see Cammy upon his release and I would appreciate it if you would give me some dates and times around the first of February for his visitation.

He was serving eighteen months in the county jail for theft. That explained his absence from the divorce hearing. Legally I had to honor his visitation request; fortunately he never followed through with it.

Cammy and I made plans to go on a one-week vacation to visit her grandparents in Florida that April. Billy arranged to join us there for the weekend and stay at his parents' condo that was also in Boca Raton.

Before we went away he asked me to make reservations at a nice restaurant for our first evening together.

The quaint Italian restaurant that my in-laws had suggested was perfect. The intimate candlelit dinner for two and glasses of red wine inspired a romantic mood for our date.

After dinner we drove to Deerfield Beach to take an evening walk along the shore. Above us the first sliver of the new moon barely illuminated the night sky. Hand-in-hand in the darkness, barefooted on the cool sand, we paused to share a kiss. Billy seized the moment. As I watched with astonishment, he slid his hand into his pocket and produced a ring. In concert with the tranquil sound of the rolling surf he proposed marriage to me. I felt like the luckiest girl in the world!

He handed the engagement ring to me and I placed it on my finger. It fit perfectly! The darkness of night obscured the true beauty of the diamond. I pulled him by the hand, leading him toward the nearest streetlight. Once illuminated, the large round diamond's facets sparkled brilliantly. Stupefied by its magnificence, I asked him if it was real! He assured me it was.

My chivalrous fiancé had another surprise in store. The next day he proposed to Cammy. He told her how much he loved her and wanted to be her Daddy, and then gave her a tiny diamond "engagement ring" too! The deal was sealed. He had captured our hearts forever.

As far as Billy was concerned, Cammy was his daughter. Now that we planned to get married he wanted to adopt her and make it legal. I wanted nothing more for both of them, but there was no way that Keith would ever consent to forfeiting his parental rights. Even though he had no interactions with her, Cammy was his lifeline; if he lost his daughter he'd surely die from a broken heart.

When we began discussing our wedding plans, Billy's parents had one request. They asked me to obtain a Jewish divorce called a *get*, so we could be married by their rabbi in their Orthodox synagogue.

According to ancient Jewish law a couple remains married until the woman receives the *get*.

Without a *get*, marrying another man is considered adulterous and her children would be considered illegitimate. The initiation of the divorce must come from the husband. Keith was so far gone by that time; the only thing he could capably do was get loaded. It would have been ludicrous to ask him to initiate a Jewish divorce. Exceptions could be made under certain circumstances; I hoped drug addiction fell under that category.

It's not every day that a girl gets a *get*! Only a rabbinical court can authorize a Jewish divorce. After consulting with Billy's family rabbi, I called to discuss my dilemma with his suggested referral. The woman who answered the phone passed my message on to the head rabbi for a determination. He decided that my circumstances warranted an exception and agreed to perform the ceremony. The woman called me back to schedule an appointment. The *get* ceremony was to be performed at that rabbi's home in an ultra-pious section of Baltimore City.

I hadn't the foggiest idea about what to expect when I arrived there. A religious looking, bearded older man wearing a black suit answered the door. He invited me into the house by extending his hand toward the center of the room. He never touched me or uttered a word. A handful of other rabbinical looking men, all in black suits and bearded, were waiting inside.

As I met each of their glances they nodded then looked away. Though I felt like a leper, their behavior was founded in respect. The Torah prohibits observant men from touching or gazing at women other than their wives or relatives. The law recognizes that the physical attraction between men and women is instinctive. The ban prevents men from lustful sin by distancing them from temptation.

Once they got started the men, speaking only in Hebrew, role-played for awhile. One man held a rolled up paper document in his hand. I got the impression that he represented my husband. Suddenly he started scolding me in Hebrew and literally threw the document at me! I had no idea what he said to me, but once the *get* was in my possession my Jewish divorce was official. The procedure was rudely chauvinistic but I left the house a free woman.

Billy and I got busy planning our wedding. We wanted an intimate ceremony and celebration; neither of us liked a lot of fanfare. I'd already been down that road and Billy was a very private person. Anxious to tie the knot, we chose Thursday, July 28th as our wedding date. That didn't give us much time to make the arrangements.

We limited our guest list to fifty people, including only family and close friends. Our ceremony would be held at Beth Tfiloh synagogue in the beautiful glass-walled chapel. For our reception we chose the banquet room at Peerce's Plantation, a lovely restaurant in a country setting. We planned a four-day, three-night honeymoon to the Dutch/Caribbean Island of St. Maarten/Saint Martin. Neither one of us could stand to be away from Cammy any longer than that.

I bought myself a cameo-colored satin and lace dress to wear as the bride and had a short veil made to match it. Cammy's dress was a pastel floral princess-style with a white eyelet neckline and a pink satin ribbon that tied around her waist. I bought silver Maryjane shoes for her to wear on her teensy feet. Along with the rest of my floral order, I had a small wreath of pink sweetheart roses and baby's breath made for her hair and a matching nosegay for her to carry.

After maintaining separate residences I broke my lease, and Cammy and I moved into Billy's house at The Falls. The move was only temporary though; we were looking for a new house to buy together.

Cammy wasn't feeling well on our wedding day but she didn't let on. As we posed for our formal photos before the ceremony I heard her little voice getting raspy. She was such a good little girl, trying her best to force a smile for the photographer. She never once complained the entire day.

As our guests were arriving, Billy, Cammy, and I sat down in the rabbi's study to sign our *Ketubah*. The *Ketubah* is an integral part of a traditional Jewish marriage; the signing of the document by the intended bride and groom precedes the nuptials. Just as we began, Cammy asked Billy to take her to the bathroom. We were busy with the *Ketubah* ceremony so when he didn't respond quickly enough she began pestering him. She wouldn't let up and the rabbi was unable to continue. He paused and offered his private bathroom. Billy got up and took her. The rabbi impatiently paced back and forth behind his desk the entire time they were in there. After a few minutes he wisecracked, "Come on you two!" Our videographer captured the entire comical episode.

With the *Ketubah* signed and our guests seated, Billy, Cammy, and I listened outside the sanctuary for our musical cue. Cammy, excited with anticipation, peered through the long glass windows of the chapel's double doors. When we heard our song play, the three of us entered the chapel and proceeded down the aisle together. Cammy stole the spotlight, self-assuredly sauntering ahead of us, flashing smiles from side to side to all our guests. Only three years old, she really knew how to work a crowd!

She looked angelic with the floral wreath nestled in the halo of her golden curls. When we reached the end of the aisle, my father lifted her up so she could see everybody and then sat her down on his lap. Billy and I continued, ascending the steps of the *bimah* to the *chuppah* for our wedding ceremony.

The rabbi spoke touchingly about our relationship and our families. He explained the extraordinary significance of our Hebrew wedding date, the fifteenth day in the month of *Av*. According to the Talmud, on that particular date in history, boys and girls of Jerusalem would go out to find a mate. He said that beautiful marriages were traditionally made on that day. Standing under the *chuppah*, ready to be joined in holy matrimony, God gave us confirmation of what we already knew. Destiny brought us together and 'til death would we part.

Forty-One: A Soft Place to Land

It's so easy to fall in love
but hard to find someone
who will catch you.
~ Author Unknown

Although sizable, the Jewish community of Baltimore is unusually close knit; everybody knows each other or knows someone who knows them. The Jewish people of my parents' generation grew up nestled together in specific Baltimore City neighborhoods. As a group, they began migrating north to the county in the late 1950's. My generation grew up in or near the Pikesville/Randallstown areas, the Jewish hubs of Baltimore County. In the 1980's the yuppie Pikesvillians of my age group were beginning to migrate farther north toward a rural suburb of the county called Owings Mills.

When we started searching for a home to buy we focused our attention on Owings Mills. New housing developments were just beginning to spring up on the farmlands that had previously blanketed that hilly area. We looked at some resale houses but ideally wanted to build a brand new one.

Our search led us to the model homes of a brand new community called Velvet Hills South. The modern-looking homes had the stained wooden exterior siding that was all the rage in the 1980's and 90's. We picked out a corner lot and decided on a model that we could afford to buy. The builder was easy to work with and very flexible with customization. Before taking a deposit, they encouraged us to meet with their architect to discuss the interior changes we wanted to make. Everything fell into place, and we signed a contract with them to build our brand new house.

Billy visited the house nearly every day from the first time the lot markers went in the ground to the day we moved in. Not only was he a perfectionist, he understood every aspect of the building process and was naturally proficient in many of them. From November 6, 1988 to April 20, 1989 he kept a detailed daily journal and took photographs of each task completed. I'm glad he had his eye on the ball because I was clueless.

Decorating the new house was challenging; our tastes were miles apart. A palate of black, red, and silver had dominated Billy's professionally decorated townhouse. Except for a black leather sectional sofa and red and chrome Bruer chairs, his furniture had been custom built. The look well suited a bachelor's pad but I personally hated those colors. The light blue, beige and mauve suite rescued from Cliffedge Road was my only contribution. That fit perfectly in the formal living room. We agreed on a combination of purple, silver, and black for the rest of the house.

For Cammy's bedroom I selected shades of lavender, with her twin-size brass bed serving as the focal point. I repainted my childhood white French provincial furniture in very pale lavender to coordinate with the silk Victorian-style wallpaper behind it. Though she was only three years old, I chose a décor that I thought would remain relevant for a teenage girl.

I had to pinch myself. I was living the "white picket fence" fantasy…minus the fence. In Billy I had found stability, among many other amazing qualities. If I had to describe him in one word I would have said "normal." Drama did not prevail in his world. I didn't know people like that even walked the earth. Sure, he had his quirks like everyone else; I'm definitely not calling him perfect. But he was a smart guy with his head on straight, a heart of gold, and his feet planted firmly on the ground.

For the first time in twenty-nine years I'd found a soft place to land. Though I'd never consciously deliberated upon it, I believed without reservation that Billy would catch me if I fell or run my life if I couldn't. I'd never trusted someone as unequivocally as I trusted my husband.

Little did I suspect that in the comfort of his security, safe and sound at last, the festering emotional stockpile I'd internalized for years would rupture. My body, suddenly overcome by the surge of emancipated poison, fell apart.

My digestive system was the first order of attack. Trying to avoid the discomfort I felt after eating, I drastically reduced my food intake. That resulted in substantial weight loss, then overwhelming fatigue. I consulted with doctors who ran all sorts of tests including a colonoscopy and endoscopy but found nothing medically wrong. They attributed my symptoms to stress but offered no concrete solutions.

When I lost faith in the medical community I turned toward a holistic approach. Desperation led me to a crackpot "healer" that had his own smorgasbord of problems. In addition to his kooky regimens and the recommendation of questionable herbs, he practiced the laying of hands on me. I was unaware that his own disharmony could be passed to me by negative energy flowing through his hands. He recommended another practitioner to cleanse my system through high colonics. The colonics rapidly depleted my already low electrolyte levels and I got much worse. My muscles became so weak I couldn't get out of bed.

Billy watched me get progressively sicker. A logical problem-solver, he felt helpless in the face of my illusive disorder. He supported me through all the trials and errors and took over for me when I couldn't function. His devotion to his new bride never wavered.

I suffered for many months, resolving one issue only to have a new one surface. I began experiencing random panic attacks causing severe hyperventilation that felt like suffocation. Those episodes were terrifying.

My first crisis followed the painting of our house interior. At the time I believed that my breathing difficulty was an allergic reaction to the fresh paint. When I began gasping for air Billy called 911. The E.M.T.'s arriving on the scene, also assuming my reaction was allergic, gave me oxygen and a shot of Epinephrine. When my breathing didn't improve, they rushed me to the hospital emergency room by ambulance. On the way there they injected me two more times with Epinephrine. My anxiety level went through the roof and I still felt like I couldn't get any air into my lungs.

After having already worked a sixteen-hour shift, the intern that examined me in the E.R. treated me like I was psychotic. His bedside manner was atrocious. He insisted that nothing was wrong with my breathing and told me to stop acting crazy. That only exacerbated my anxiety, provoking me to scream like a Banshee and upset the entire emergency room. A nurse came running in with a paper bag for me to breathe into. That did the trick. After a few more scary episodes a doctor identified my breathing difficulties as panic attacks and taught me relaxation techniques. The seeming lack of air was from too much oxygen, not too little.

My search for wellness eventually led me to healing through the practice of acupuncture and traditional Chinese medicine. The primary function of the ancient art is regulation of the qi circulation (vital energy), to assist the body in self-healing. When a qi meridian is blocked, the body becomes unbalanced. Acupuncture opens the blockages, stimulates the immune system, and balances the emotions. I've never found a gentler, more comprehensive approach to healing. Acupuncture and Chinese medicine have remained an integral part of my wellbeing ever since.

Terribly difficult at times, that first challenge so early in our marital life only served to make us stronger as a couple. Our commitment to each other was unshakeable.

Forty-Two: Fourth of July

Life is eternal, and love is immortal, and death is only a horizon; and a horizon is nothing save the limit of our site.
~Rossiter   Worthington Raymond

Keith's maternal grandmother was his only living grandparent. Oblivious to their drug problems, she thought the sun rose and set with her two grandsons. Keith's grandfather had passed away many years before, leaving his grandmother very well off. She lived frugally off of her social security income, and never enjoyed her wealth.

Keith's mother was an only child. His parents had carefully managed his grandmother's money and planned her will. They didn't want nor need the inheritance; they just aimed at preventing their drug addicted sons from squandering it. The brothers believed that they'd split her money when she died but they didn't know the exact terms of the will.

Keith genuinely loved his Grandma. She lived in Florida so he made sure to call her once a week. Mike, incapable of love, only buttered her up for the money.

Keith believed that Mike wanted him dead; without Keith, Mike thought he'd inherit their grandmother's entire estate. Knowing the snake Keith was dealing with I never doubted his logic for a second; Mike had plotted against him their entire lives.

Certain that Keith wouldn't have the willpower to resist, Mike would often hand him enough pills to overdose. Near the end of his life, Keith told his friend that he was sure that Mike was trying to kill him.

In the back of my mind I always worried that Mike would eventually come looking for Cammy since she would be Keith's only heir. To protect her we had an unlisted telephone number and kept my last name hidden from him.

Fortunately through my marriage to Billy, Cammy and I gained a wonderful new family. Billy's family was wholesome and remarkably close. His parents were warm, generous, loving people who had raised three outstanding children. Billy, his sister, and his brother were each other's best friends. And that family bond extended to all their relatives also. I'd never seen anything like it. Billy's family loved Cammy as deeply as if she were their own flesh and blood.

Even though we never heard from or saw Keith, my relationship with his parents remained close. It was confusing for me at first dividing my new loyalties to Billy's parents from the loyalties I still had with my ex in-laws. The two families were polar opposites with nothing in common except their love for Cammy. With Cammy so young I took it upon myself to nurture both of those relationships for her. The paths of the two families never had occasions to cross, but I tread softly with each relationship, worried that I might accidentally offend somebody. It was still my nature to please everyone in my life.

My daughter, the only grandchild of three sets of doting grandparents, was showered with a plethora of love and attention. The abundance she had in her life was far more than I could have ever wished for or dreamed possible. These were gifts sent from heaven...perhaps under the watchful eyes of Winnie and Bobitz! Keith and I were the vessels that brought her here, but God clearly had a plan for his child.

I prayed that Keith wouldn't someday reenter Cammy's life and turn her world upside down. She had no conscious memory of him so she felt no emotional attachment or loss. Billy was the only Daddy she'd ever known and loved.

From a very early age I kept an open dialogue with Cammy about Keith by sharing stories and showing her pictures. I explained that her first Daddy loved her very much but was too sick to be a part of her life. The older she got the more detailed my explanations became. Although I saw no indication of an addictive personality, I wanted her to have a clear understanding of the nature of addiction in case she was genetically predisposed.

Billy and I discussed having a second child. We both wanted a baby even though he said he'd be perfectly content with Cammy as his only child. I'd always pictured myself with two children though I wasn't anxious to suffer through the debilitating sickness of pregnancy again. With Cam out of diapers and fairly self-sufficient at four years old, I finally had achieved some independence. But at thirty, I didn't want to become too complacent before starting over with a newborn. We decided to start trying, knowing with my history that it could take several months for me to conceive. Since I already had a daughter, I hoped for a son.

Cammy had just completed the four-year-old private preschool program. We looked forward to her starting Kindergarten at our districted school Timber Grove Elementary in the fall. Summer was upon us once again. That meant a trip or two to Bethany Beach, Delaware to stay in my in-law's condo at Sea Colony. Sometimes we planned our trip around the July fourth weekend; Bethany Beach always had a parade during the day and fireworks on the beach at night. That year we decided to celebrate the holiday at home. Our friends were having an afternoon party at their house and we planned to take Cammy to the park to watch the fireworks later on.

Independence Day fell on a Wednesday that year. July had been an unusually rainy month but luckily the weather held out for the holiday. To assure parking and a space to spread out our camp we had to arrive at the park a couple hours early. We gathered up a soft, worn-in comforter, snacks, drinks, and a few card games, and left home after six o'clock. The fireworks usually began around nine, just after dark. To keep Cammy occupied we brought along her favorite card game, a Garfield version of Go Fish. She loved playing that game over and over.

As darkness gradually blanketed the summer sky, the three of us waited with eager anticipation for the pageantry to begin. Suddenly we heard the familiar-sounding resonant boom, followed by a magnificent burst of shimmering colors that lit up the sky. Thousands of patriotic spectators applauded enthusiastically.

We hadn't a care in the world; the three of us snuggled together under the stars on that warm summer night. The future looked bright for our little family of three, maybe four someday. Our life together was just beginning. We were happy.

But all wasn't right with the world that night. I had no idea what awaited me at home.

When the three of us walked into our house later that night I saw the light on the answering machine blinking. I pushed the button and listened to the startling message that Keith's mother had left for me. I called her back before I'd even had a chance to fully absorb the implication of her words.

Keith's mother explained that he had suffered a fatal overdose. His brother found him unresponsive that morning in his bed; the exact time of death was unknown. On July 4, 1990, at thirty-four years old, Keith's tortured soul was finally called home to rest. He'd reached his journey's end.

According to the autopsy report, his cause of death was intoxication from an acute combination of Methadone, Cyclobenzaprine (Flexeril), and Promethazine (Phenergan). The imminence of his early death did not prepare me for its impact. I took it hard.

Forty-Three: Meant to Be

Life is not measured by the number of breaths we take, but by the number of moments that take our breath away.
~ Author Unknown

B illy waited a respectable six months after Keith's passing to begin adoption proceedings. On April 26, 1991 Cammy became Billy's daughter in the eyes of the law. She was five years old. Of course they didn't need that document to prove the depth of their love for one another. He had always been her beloved Daddy and she his precious daughter. We'd all made a pact...it was meant to be.

Epilogue

On September 17, 1991 I gave birth to our second child, a son that we named Kerry. The years have flown by; Kerry is now nineteen years old and in his sophomore year of college. He is a handsome guy; tall and thin with gorgeous blue eyes. Billy and I are so proud of the intelligent, talented, and level-headed young man that he's grown up to be. He has a very bright future ahead of him.

Cammy is now twenty-five years old. There aren't enough words of praise to describe the remarkable woman that she has become. She has given her family constant joy and pride since the day she was born. Her inner beauty radiates like a golden aura around her as do her tresses of long, blonde, curly hair.

After eight consecutive semesters on the University's Dean's list, she graduated Magna Cum Laude in 2007 with a degree in finance. She's gifted in mathematics and has narrowed down her passion to the field of Statistics. Cammy's intelligence, maturity, and forthright character have rapidly advanced her as a professional in her career.

Although Keith never finished high school he was extraordinarily gifted in math, and calculating statistics was his favorite pastime. Astoundingly he passed all of his positive traits on to Cammy and none of his deficiencies.

Cammy has no recollection of ever having known her biological father, though she knows everything about him. She's never felt a loss. Billy was, is, and will forever be her wonderful Daddy.

Cammy is the only grandchild Keith's parents ever had. They've maintained a very close relationship through the years. She is all the family they have left. Keith's brother died in 2009 at fifty-nine years old of unknown, drug related causes. Except for limited and occasional contact with his father he'd been mostly estranged from his parents for many years. For reasons mentioned in my book Cammy never knew him.

My ex in-laws continue to deeply grieve the loss of their two sons. They ask themselves where they went wrong as parents. Keith's mother has not left the confines of her Florida condo for anything other than the most necessary appointments in two years. Her body remains alive but her spirit is forever gone.

Billy and my ex in-laws have grown very fond of each other. And in the past five years Billy's parents have embraced Keith's parents as family too. Though the two families share little else in common, their love for Cammy has bound them together.

Billy and I have been happily married for twenty-two years. He is an extraordinary husband and father; I couldn't have dreamed a more perfect man into my life. I am truly blessed.

My awareness of God's presence in my life is constant. I thank him often for the gifts he continues to grace me with, large and small. It seems the more grateful I am, the more miracles he performs in my life.

A light went off in my head about two years ago, prompting me to call the Baltimore County Police Department and inquire about the status of the evidence from my 1980 rape case. I wondered if traces of DNA might be present and could be used as an investigative tool. The detective that I spoke with told me that my property had unfortunately been discarded. It was 2008; in the early eighties they knew nothing about DNA profiling and therefore didn't have the foresight to hold on to the evidence.

I had made the call without any expectations of the outcome so was not at all disappointed. I knew that the likelihood of finding the perpetrator of my crime thirty years later was no greater than it had been when my case was still fresh.

Then in the spring of 2009 I received a telephone call, unprompted and unrelated to my call the year before, from a Baltimore County cold-case detective who had located me. He respectfully eased into the reason for his call, understandably concerned with stirring up the pain of my past.

He explained that the cold-case department had stumbled upon an amazing discovery. They'd located all the pathological slides that the doctor who'd examined me thirty years ago had ever collected at the GBMC Rape Crisis Center. The doctor had brilliantly saved the evidence from every rape crime that he had processed going as far back as the 1970's. The detective told me that they'd already reviewed my case for legitimacy as well as confirmed the presence of two sets of DNA evidence from my slide.

Most women he'd talked to had no interest in emotionally revisiting their attack; I on the other hand was elated. The detective let me know how relieved he was by my positive reaction.

On my approval he networked with the police department in the county where I currently reside. Together they arranged for a DNA swab sample from my mouth to be collected and sent the Baltimore County Crime Lab.

To determine the perpetrator's DNA they needed to identify and subtract my DNA code from the mix. But the final result would only be beneficial if the rapist had been charged with a crime after 1994 and consequently entered into the Maryland DNA Database. What were the odds of that happening?

The detective thought that we'd have an outcome in six weeks, but five months passed without any results. In the interim, a female detective took over my case. She stayed in contact with me while we both waited, anxiously and impatiently, for word from the lab.

In November of 2009, after waiting six months for results, I received a call from the detective. She told me that the DNA results had finally come back from the lab and the Maryland DNA Database had been searched for a match.

The news was good; they had identified the perpetrator! He was already being held in the county jail after having recently been implicated by a different detective through the same process, but in a different rape case.

I'd always known that I'd been lucky but had never realized just how lucky until I learned about his other victim.

The other rape he'd been charged with, also through DNA profiling, had been very violent. The fifty-eight year old victim had fought for her life. He had beaten her up and broken her ribs. Then he had tied her hands together, tied a rope around her neck, and hung her upside down in a closet. He robbed her house and left her for dead. The rope had cut into her throat so deeply that her muscles and larynx were exposed. She managed to untie her hands, break loose, and crawl out of the closet. She was bleeding profusely when her thirty-three year old son luckily came home and found her. Unbelievably, she survived and lived well into her eighties.

Unfortunately the woman never lived to see her attacker identified and arrested. The only witness to her attack was her son, who could testify only to what he saw after the fact.

Since I was the only surviving witness, the Assistant State's Attorney determined that I had the stronger case to try him on. She had already charged the man with twelve counts in the other woman's case. Within days of linking him to my crime she officially charged him with four counts in my assault. With my approval she planned to prosecute him to the fullest extent of the law; a maximum life sentence.

As the story unfolded I learned that he was a serial rapist; he had actually raped three women in the span of fourteen months. I was the first, the woman that he'd left for dead was the second, and a woman who was later able to identify and prosecute him was the third. In the early 1980's he'd received a thirty year sentence for the third woman's crime. He only served ten years then was paroled. The legal system knew nothing about his other two victims at that time. There were no similarities in the three cases; age of victim, location, or otherwise. How he chose his victims was never determined.

On February 24, 2010, under the advisement of his court-appointed attorney, he chose to enter a guilty plea to one count of first degree rape in my case. He'd been backed into a corner; DNA evidence is considered indisputable proof. By pleading guilty, he no longer had to face a jury and be tried on all four counts.

On May 20, 2010, the day of his sentencing in court, I had the opportunity to directly face the man who had raped me thirty years prior. He looked right at me and listened intently as I read my emotionally-charged victim's impact statement. He was so engrossed in what I was saying; it was as if my voice from thirty years ago was now haunting him. This is what I said:

> *I want you to know about the girl you violated thirty years ago and the impact that your heinous actions had on my life.*
> *I was twenty-one years old at the time and looking forward to celebrating my twenty-second birthday in a few weeks I'd been living on my own for two years. I was young, carefree, and enjoying*

my newly achieved independence. Life was fun and exciting; I had everything to look forward to. Although my roommate and I hadn't known each other when I'd first moved into her apartment, we had become very close friends and were happy living together. Everything changed the night you broke into my home while I soundly slept, terrorized me in my bedroom, threatened my life and raped me.

You were nothing but a coward that night. You deliberately isolated me, leaving me defenseless without any possible way to escape. I couldn't even scream; you held a knife against my throat and I intensely feared for my life. No one was around, and no one would have heard me or could have come to my rescue in time to save me. I didn't know who you were or the degree of your perversion. I didn't know if you possessed even a shred or moral fiber or were psychopathic. And I didn't know if I would live through the night or if you planned to kill me after you'd had your way with me.

*You confessed your diabolical plan to me; you told me how you had stalked me and premeditated the attack. How you had been watching me while I unknowingly relaxed outside of my apartment building and talked to my neighbors, naively enjoying my young life. It was a terrifying nightmare that I prayed I'd wake up from…only it **was** real, I **was** awake.*

You callously took what you wanted from me without the slightest concern of the way in which your evil-minded actions would impact the rest of my life. I suspect that you've gone on with your life and never looked back. Thank God I kept a pillow over my head and never saw your face that night. At least I didn't have the horrifying vision of your evil face haunting me for the last thirty years. But my other senses had become heightened, and to this day I remember every detail as if it had happened yesterday. My whole life fell apart after that night. Besides the residual terror I felt, I was an emotional wreck. I lashed out at my roommate and moved out shortly after. We've never spoken again. I went into a deep depression and fell on hard times. I isolated myself from friends. Out of despair and confusion, I made some very bad choices in my life.

Not a night has passed in the last thirty years that I haven't woken up between 2 a.m. and 4 a.m., looked at my alarm clock, and remembered what you did to me. That memory will never be erased; it is deeply imbedded in my mind. You stole my right and my ability to feel comfortable alone. Your selfish invasion of my private space thirty years ago has left me feeling forever vulnerable to another attack. I refuse to sleep without the protection of a house alarm, worried that I will once again awake from a sound sleep to an unwelcome and menacing intruder in my bedroom. I'll never again enjoy the cool breeze of the night air through my open bedroom window while I sleep, and have never allowed my children to sleep with their windows open either for fear that someone like you will harm us. That fear will remain with me until the day I die. I will not walk into a home or a building alone unless an alarm system proves to me that no one has entered before me and could *be lying in wait. These are the things you forever stole from me that night. I feel vindicated that you've been caught and pray that you will never again have the opportunity to ruin another life.*

The man had the opportunity to read his own statement. He continually sobbed as he admitted his crime. He faced me and my family, apologized for the pain he'd caused us, and asked for forgiveness.

The judge sentenced him to life in prison for his crime against me. Already sixty years old, the man will die in prison.

The solving of my case is nothing short of a miracle. We all experience miracles; some are just more obvious than others.

I now live a peaceful, joyous, drama free life and cherish every minute of it. I gratefully awake each morning with an open mind and an open heart, ready to experience all that life has to offer. And I can't wait to see what's around the next corner...whatever that may be.